Prai~

Only God chronicles the lives of two ordinary individuals who chose to live out an extraordinary life of faith and, as a result, became vessels of God used to transform thousands of lives. As Larry and Jean Johnson's pastor for many years, it was my honor to watch their journey unfold up close. *Only God* tells the story of God's provision, direction, grace, and power as Larry and Jean choose to fully trust in Him. The seeds sown through their ministry, Will Go Inc., will continue to bring forth fruit for decades to come. The events recounted in this book have the potential to transform generations of people all over the world. Who is capable of using lives in such a way? Only God!

Michael Carmody
Pastor, adjunct professor of religion, ICCC
Author of *Triumph in the Wilderness* and
Filled with the Fullness of God

Reading *Only God* is like sitting at the table with your grandparents, listening to them share testimonies of God's grace and goodness. Once you begin reading, you can hardly put the book down. Such a great account of two lives surrendered to Jesus and His call to the people of planet Earth. This book will encourage you in your faith and in your confidence that only God can direct our steps and order our paths.

Pastor RJ Ciaramitaro

Only God tells of the inspirational journey of a faith-filled couple who lived a life of love, service, adventure, and obedience to God. This fast-moving book will make you laugh, cry, and fall to your knees in worship. From the fields of Iowa to being guided by God's audible voice to a revival in a Buddhist monastery to having a documentary about their ministry broadcast on national TV by a communist government, this book shows how Jesus shaped and used this humble, care-motivated, take-action duo. Saturated with Scripture, each story brings the Bible to life. Along with the high times, this book speaks honestly of Larry and Jean's failures, disappointments, and struggles to stay true in difficulty. Through it all, you see what God can do through vessels who are yielded to Him. If only there were more Larry and Jean Johnsons in the world. I widely recommend this book for everyone.

Dr. Rich Kao, pastor, author of *Caring Deeply about Church Planting*

My husband Eric and I have known Larry and Jean for many years and have been blessed to watch God's faithfulness operate through their ministry Will Go Inc. The Johnsons are the real deal! In Jean's words, "God works through people. We believe relationships are vital for the furtherance of God's Kingdom." Now in *Only God*, the Johnsons' story will inspire your faith and show you how much can be accomplished when we partner with God and others in loving, committed relationships and a unified vision!

Amy Robnik Joob
Speaker, life coach, and author of *Model Behavior* and *Unstuck: Step into the New*

Your heart will be greatly encouraged as Larry and Jean share story after story of the faithfulness of God. Nothing is impossible for Him, as seen clearly in these pages. Testimony after testimony speaks about the wonders of what God is doing among His beloved people. *Only God* will encourage you to pursue the plans and dreams He has placed in your heart. If you are willing to say yes and trust in Him, He is faithful.

Bethany Mailloux
Lover and follower of Jesus

What a joy and privilege to count Larry and Jean Johnson as friends for over three decades. *Only God* is a record of what the Lord can do through anyone who says, "Lord, we will go," regardless of ages or finances. With humor and courage, Larry and Jean tell riveting stories of God's faithfulness sure to inspire you to listen to the voice of Jesus and go carry out the Great Commission. These stirring stories of the Johnsons' love boomeranging all around the world will make you want to fasten your seatbelts and let your heart cry, "Here am I, Lord. Send me!"

Dave and Jeanne Kaufman
Pastors, authors of *White-Knuckle Faith:*
Trusting God in Times of Crisis

ONLY GOD

ONLY GOD

A TESTIMONY OF GOD'S GOODNESS
FROM THE *Cornfields* OF *Iowa* TO
THE *Harvest Fields* OF THE *World*

A Memoir

Larry and Jean Johnson

REDEMPTION PRESS

Published by Redemption Press, PO Box 427, Enumclaw, WA 98022.

Toll-Free (844) 2REDEEM (273-3336)

Redemption Press is honored to present this title in partnership with the author. The views expressed or implied in this work are those of the author. Redemption Press provides our imprint seal representing design excellence, creative content, and high-quality production.

The author has tried to recreate events, locales, and conversations from memories of them. In order to maintain their anonymity, in some instances the names of individuals, some identifying characteristics, and some details may have been changed, such as physical properties, occupations, and places of residence.

ISBN 13: 978-1-64645-596-6 (Paperback)
978-1-64645-595-9 (ePub)
978-1-64645-594-2 (Mobi)

Library of Congress Catalog Card Number: 2022918158

To our grandchildren, Hayley, Jaden, and Hannah Johnson. May the words of this book help to propel you into the purposes and plans God has ordained for each of your lives. Amen.

Contents

Acknowledgments

This book could not have been written without each of you whom God divinely placed by our side. This is a team story, and all glory goes to *only God*.

We also want to thank the staff of Redemption Press who carefully helped us shape, write, edit, and publish this book. Athena Dean Holtz, Tisha Martin, Dori Harrell, and Mari Gonzales were key. Thanks also to independent editor Becky Skillin who assisted us in the initial stages of our manuscript. The old adage "better together" certainly applies here.

To our children, Larry Jr., Angela and Clay Sandburg, and Jared and Heather Johnson, who always provided an open door, encouragement, and prayers. We hope you know that because of your multiple helps, we were able to freely walk through the doors God opened to us. Words cannot convey our gratefulness—God knew what He was doing when He gave us you!

Introduction

Finally, brethren, whatever things are true, whatever things are noble, whatever things are just, whatever things are pure, whatever things are lovely, whatever things are of good report, if there is any virtue and if there is anything praiseworthy—meditate on these things.

Philippians 4:8

September 28, 2020: We began writing this account during a world pandemic. The year 2020 turned into a series of years no one could have envisioned and will be remembered by its extraordinary events: COVID-19 with its millions of cases and more than a million deaths; George Floyd's last words, "I can't breathe"; rioting from Portland to Toronto; international tensions; and of course, the drama and real-life situations around the presidential elections in the USA. As if all this were not enough, many families, including ours, have experienced their own personal traumas. Just this year, our oldest son was diagnosed with thyroid cancer and faced numerous tests and procedures. Friends and family have lost lifelong mates and countless others have faced extreme financial hardship. It seems the teeter-totter is heavy on the negative end.

However, amid the heaviness and harsh realities of life, God's light and peace continued to break through. September

26, 2020: Peaceful assembly of 15,000 Christians from all fifty states gracing the National Mall in Washington, DC; testimonies of coronavirus survivors; God illuminating the need for social change in police departments and justice systems; and churches and ministries prayerfully providing helps all around the world. In the entertainment spotlight, Brandon Leake won America's Got Talent 2020. He introduced spoken word poetry to us all. His last performance began with the song "Jesus Loves Me."

Hope is surely alive.

In the light of all these things, Larry and I felt it was time to reflect on the goodness of God—to tell the stories of Jesus and His mighty acts through our lives. As you read these accounts, you will distinctly see two things at work.

Only by God's divine intervention could these things take place.

God works through people. We believe relationships are vital for the furtherance of God's kingdom.

The Formative Years
LARRY

CHAPTER 1

Hello, World

Direct your children onto the right path, and
when they are older, they will not leave it.

Proverbs 22:6 NLT

> Through the trials and sometimes hardships of growing up, two principles remain key. They are the love and care of parents and guidance toward faith in Jesus Christ. Not only do everyday routines and events bring joys known only to a child, but they also set the character blocks of life.

On June 28, 1943, I was born at home on our Iowa farm, the seventh child of Lawrence and Lillian Mae Henderson Johnson. Three additional siblings were born after me. All of us children were raised on that 120-acre farm. And because of Dad and Mom's disciplined, conservative ways, the farm was paid off and never lost during tough times.

My parents' example showed me and my siblings the value of hard work. Mom canned hundreds of quarts of vegetables each year from our garden. I didn't appreciate the fact that we were eating organically grown foods; I wished for store bought. With so many of us to care for, she kept a weekly routine. Monday was wash day. All the clothes were washed in a wringer washing machine and hung outside on clotheslines to dry. In winter, clothes hung throughout the house on wooden racks. Ironing was always needed. Sometimes I ironed my own jeans and shirts for basketball games or dates as Mom had more to do than one lady could handle. We all had chores, both inside and out. We four brothers shared one of the upstairs bedrooms, sleeping in two double beds. We were to make sure our beds were made and clothes put away. Outside, Dad kept about a dozen milk cows. Each morning before school, it was my job to milk them. I think he really did need my help, because as soon as I graduated from high school, he sold them.

My parents were very frugal, never upgrading or buying extras unless they had the cash. That conservatism meant we were behind our neighbors in the comfort department. We didn't have running water until I was twelve years old, and I was sixteen before we bought our first television. We were a close family and knew our parents loved us. However, kids being kids, we didn't always behave well, especially us boys; so it was a dedicated effort on my parents' part to "direct your children onto the right path" as Proverbs 22:6 (NLT) instructs. Each Sunday, they loaded us up in the '49 Woody station wagon and took us to the Congregational church for Sunday school and church.

I still remember Pastor Nettleton stopping by to pick us kids up for Vacation Bible School. My mother never learned to drive, so it was his kindness that allowed us to go. Our spiritual lives were being formed. One of my Sunday school teachers gave me a picture of Jesus standing at the door, knocking ("The Light of the World" by William Holman Hunt 1827–1910). She told us there was not a handle on the door because it could only be opened from the inside. We had to let Jesus in. For several years, I carried that picture with me almost everywhere I went. I believe that God was touching my heart even then.

In my early years, I enjoyed school. I remember learning to read—"See Sally run. Look at Jack jumping."—and about Dick getting on the bus to go to school. I remember learning the alphabet, printing letters, adding and subtracting, and of course, playing with friends. School was a happy time.

But that changed when I entered sixth grade. We had a very cruel teacher, Mrs. G, who must have felt that she had to make an example out of someone to keep all the students in line. Being the biggest in the class, it seemed I was at the top of her hit list.

The first time she approached me, she said loudly, "I don't care if your dad is on the school board," and slapped me several times. My parents had impressed on us kids that if we got in trouble at school, we would be in more trouble at home. Though not necessarily true, that's what I thought. It was a living nightmare. Almost habitually, Mrs. G shouted demeaning words as she slapped my face, hit me on the head, or pulled my ears. I never knew when the attack would come, only that it would! I checked out and sat frozen most of the time, waiting.

It was recess time, and once again Mrs. G required me to stay inside. After all my classmates had left the room, she asked me to come to the desk because she had something for me. I was wary but obediently approached her desk. She was sucking loudly on a root beer lifesaver candy. It smelled good, and I was a little hungry.

She opened her desk draw and said, "Larry, reach down and take one."

Of course, I wanted the candy; however, as I reached toward her drawer, I heard a distinct voice say, "Don't do it."

I pulled my hand back and simply said, "No, thank you," as I retreated to my desk. No one else was in the room. I believe she would have slammed the drawer on my fingers and accused me of attempting to steal from her desk. If she really wanted to give me a candy, she would have taken it out and offered it to me.

Though I didn't realize it at the time, God was beginning to teach me to hear His voice.

Because of my anxiety and fear of Mrs. G and the loneliness and isolation I felt from most of my classmates, I often hid in the ditch until the school bus went by. Other days, I played sick. Before the year ended, I had missed over twenty-one days of school. My report card reflected the story. I had to repeat the sixth grade.

I'd faced so much abuse and rejection that I never wanted to go to school again. Hatred had built in my heart. I felt that if Mrs. G hit me again, I would kill her. But God again stood in the gap for me. Mrs. G. became very sick and missed the whole first semester. We had a wonderful substitute teacher. I was just beginning to like school again when Mrs. G was back. Whether she didn't have the energy or old fire, I don't know, but for the first few months, she never laid a hand on me or anybody; however, I remained wary.

Then everything changed again.

A new girl joined our class. She came from a poor family and wore thick, unattractive glasses. Most days, her hair was pulled back in a ponytail. One day, unexpectedly, Mrs. G. stopped writing on the blackboard, whirled around, and yelled, "You don't chew gum in my class," and lunged toward our new classmate. Mrs. G literally lifted the girl off her seat by her hair and proceeded to drag her out to the hallway. All the time, this poor girl was screaming at the top of her lungs.

It made me sick all over again. Mrs. G never touched me again; she had a new victim.

During this time, not only was God teaching me to hear His voice, but He was also placing compassion in my heart. I began to realize that some people who are mistreated do not always deserve it, and I learned that I should not accept all things at face value. God was giving me a heart for those whom life had not given a fair shake.

Ten years after graduation we had a class reunion. The class I should have graduated with graciously invited me. And can you guess the main topic? Mrs. G. One woman admitted that she started wetting the bed at night, and others said they had nightmares, fearing the trauma of enduring another school day. Though I had not completely recognized the suffering others had experienced from Mrs. G's unpredictable actions, the most surprising moment for me came just a few years later. After receiving Jesus as my Savior, God asked me to pray for Mrs. G, and I wanted to do that. Truly, God makes everything new.

CHAPTER 2

A Wake-Up Call

*Do not remember the rebellious sins of my youth. Remember me
in the light of your unfailing love, for you are merciful, O Lord.*

Psalm 25:7 NLT

Teenagers make plenty of mistakes. From outright rebellion to wrong choices, it is sometimes a rocky path to adulthood. Only God's grace and goodness allowed us to come to maturity.

God works in ways so mysterious that we often don't see or understand them until after they have happened. During high school, God used several events and people to continue teaching me to hear His voice.

I played center on the basketball team. Whether on the home court or away, we sat in a row on the bleachers and watched the girls' game before suiting up for our own. We made quite a good-looking, clean-cut ("Leave it to Beaver") statement in our matching sport coats and ties. Jean was at every game too, as part of the cheerleading squad, and that was when she first caught my eye. Soon after, her dad needed extra help with their farming and cattle operation. I got the job.

I had worked there after school for several months but still could not summon the courage to ask her for a date. But things were about to change.

One afternoon, quite unexpectedly, Jean's little brother Karl bounded into the barn. "My sister wants you to ask her to the Valentine's Day dance," he said, "but I'm not supposed to tell you that." Just as fast as he had appeared, he disappeared. I was both relieved and elated and didn't leave the farm until I asked her to that dance! It marked the first of many events and dates during high school. Then in my senior year, we decided to go steady. Jean wore my Jostens 10-karat gold knuckle-buster class ring on a chain around her neck. I was happy. Life seemed to be going well.

But there was another side to me that Jean did not know about. Sometimes I would meet my older brothers or other friends to drink beer. One summer night, I got the scare of my life. Completely unaware I was intoxicated, I drove right past my friend's house, continued to sail through town, and ended up two miles out in the countryside at the foot of a telephone pole. As sparks flew, I miraculously staggered out and back to my friend's house. The next morning, all sobered up, I reported the accident to our local sheriff, and by God's grace, no charges were laid. That was my wake-up call. God had been working on the rough, rebellious side for some time. I needed a change, and God was already setting it up.

That August, while working part-time on Jim Mattick's construction crew, I met another teenager, Dennis Weber. On an especially hot summer night, he asked if I wanted to ride with him to Fort Dodge, our local "big city," and meet some new people. I had been waiting for an opportunity to ride in his souped-up pink and black convertible and eagerly hopped in. I had no idea that God was setting up the biggest event of my life.

We pulled up in front of a small white house where I assumed a party was in progress. To my surprise, a middle-aged woman opened the door. Though I had never met this lady before, she seemed to be waiting for me. She humbly shared the love Jesus had for me.

I could feel His presence. The God who had spoken to me those times when I was in elementary school became real to me. The God who had protected me when my car had crashed helped me realize His powerful, sustaining hand. Kneeling by her sofa, I confessed my sins and invited Jesus into my heart. I cried uncontrollably for more than an hour. I knew I had done many wrong things and needed forgiveness.

Over the next few weeks, I shared my experience with some of my friends. They thought I was acting weird with all this talk about Jesus. After several miserable encounters, I decided to keep quiet, even too afraid to share with Jean what had happened to me. Little did I know that she had had her own experience and was also afraid to share with me. God was working in both of our lives separately to bring us together in His perfect timing.

Married Years
LARRY

CHAPTER 3

A Dream Come True

Give honor to marriage, and remain faithful to one
another in marriage. God will surely judge people
who are immoral and those who commit adultery.

Hebrews 13:4 NLT

Marriage is an oxymoron; though imperfect, it is perfect. Imperfect people who commit to each other and are faithful to God have the potential for a joy-filled marriage. Many trials will come, but blessed is the wife whose husband holds the umbrella during the rain. Blessed is the husband whose wife stays under that umbrella.

I began farming on the Wilson family farm near Farnhamville, Iowa, while still in high school. My childhood dream had come true. And now my high school sweetheart, Jean, was part of that dream too. She was graduating in a few months, and I planned we'd marry soon after—or so I thought.

Sometime in late November 1962, I picked out a solitaire diamond ring and light blue jewelry box at Reed Jewelers in Rockwell City, Iowa. It remained on the back seat of my 1955 Ford Fairlane until our next date. In those days, few people locked their cars and keys remained in the ignition. Theft was uncommon.

I can't remember what we did that night. I was so focused on getting her back home and proposing. As soon as we pulled into the driveway, I reached for the jewelry box and opened it so she could see the diamond inside. The look on her face already told me the answer was not going to be what I expected!

Jean was without words, began to cry, and then finally croaked out, "I really have to think about it."

Shock, disappointment, and confusion hit my heart like a brick. I backed out of the yard slowly, trying to understand what had just happened. Had I missed some cues?

The fact that she was only seventeen and that part of her dream was to go to nursing school had not entered my mind. I waited for her answer. A few weeks later, she felt like God had given her a green light. On November 30, 1963, six months after her high school graduation, we married. God had initiated our journey.

Eleven months later, our little baby boy was born! We were so happy and excited that we named him after both of us. Larry Eugene. Two and a half years later, Angela Joan was born. We named her Angela because she was born on December 21 and looked like an angel. She was always such a good girl—well named. We took her to Christmas Eve services when she was only three days old. Jared Dean, our third child, arrived in 1974.

Box Factory Prejudice

Our honeymoon was over. Everyday life and monthly bills became a reality. Bankers would loan money for farming expenses but not for living. Unfortunately, my part-time work was not cutting it. So despite a forty-mile round trip drive, I applied for a full-time job at the Fort Dodge Container Factory.

As I entered Fort Dodge and crossed the bridge over-looking the Des Moines River, I could see the box factory sitting below me in an area called "the flats." It was the poorest part of town, and most of the people living there were African Americans. So naturally, I thought many would be working in the factory since it was right on their doorstep.

As I entered, multiple machines were noisily running at full speed. Some were making the boxes, others cutting and crimping, and still others were waxing and printing. Iowa Beef Packers (IBF) and Hormel Packing Company were the major customers. I was sent to the office where a middle-aged man sat behind a small steel desk. He seemed to be all business and got straight to the interview. He asked a lot of questions and ended with "How will you benefit our company if we hire you?"

Evidently, I said the right thing, because he told me I could start the following week on the evening shift. Next, he pushed another paper under my nose and said, "Sign it." The contract stated that any invention I might create would be the sole property of the company. What choice did I have? I signed.

As I got up to leave, his demeanor suddenly changed, and menacingly he said, "There's another thing. What do you think of [Black people]?"—only he used the N-word. Before I could even answer, his finger was in my face, and with a threatening voice, he told me, "If you ever bring one of those [N-words] down here, you'll be fired on the spot."

Although I knew his behavior and words were wrong, I felt helpless. I needed this job. I said nothing. Incidentally, a few years later, both Hormel and Iowa Beef moved out of state, forcing the closure of the box factory. A blight in Fort Dodge history was gone.

I've often thought back to that moment in light of God's Word. When Queen Esther was presented with such an injustice, her response was much different. "If I perish, I perish," she had said. Since 1965, many godly men and women have taken that same heart, changing the granite face of injustice. Hope is alive.

Though I hated factory work, it allotted me the chance to expand my farming operation. After all, my goal was to be a rich farmer. I bought bigger equipment to farm more land, built a confinement hog house to farrow and raise more pigs, and explored other small business options. Hours were spent poring over cash flow projections and finding bankers who would lend more money. I worked long days and hired more help with the expectation of more profits and more wealth. Though Jean and I both loved the farm and the freedom of our own business, God in His sovereignty had other plans for us. However, He did not release us until we learned many valuable lessons, so crucial in the years to come.

> "Who has known the mind of the Lord?
>   Or who has been his counselor?"
> "Who has ever given to God,
>   that God should repay him?"
> For from him and through him and for him are
> all things.
>   To him be the glory forever. Amen.
> (Romans 11:34–36 NIV)

CHAPTER 4

Farming

*I will send you the seasonal rains. The land will then yield
its crops, and the trees of the field will produce their fruit.*

Leviticus 26:4 NLT

> Few other occupations on earth display the power and
> glory of the Lord like farming. Who can explain a seed
> emerging from the earth to produce a crop of corn or the
> birth of twelve piglets from one mama sow? Seeing God's
> faithfulness through multiple seasons built a strong faith
> in the miraculous. We could count on Him whether on
> the mountaintop or in the valley to guide and provide.

Farming is big business and requires a lot of funding.
Every year we borrowed thousands of dollars. To secure
our loan, the bank required hail insurance to cover any crop
damage or loss. Though it was expensive, we complied.

God Speaks to Farmers
One particular year I really considered not taking the insurance but heard God say, "Cover yourself." A severe hailstorm
rolled through, wiping out some of our fields. We collected
nearly $30,000 in damages.

A few years later, I again considered buying or not buying hail insurance.

I heard God speak. "Trust me, you don't need it."

However, in late summer a severe hailstorm rolled through again. I ran outside, praying, "God, you told me to trust you. Help me."

And with my own eyes, I saw the hail come to the fence on our land and stop. Our neighbors all had significant damage.

God was building my listening ear and exercising my steadfast faith to trust His voice.

Trust in the Lord with all your heart and lean not on your own understanding; in all your ways acknowledge Him, and He shall direct your paths. (Proverbs 3:5–6)

I Missed the Bid
Farming had been financially tough for many farmers. To help, the US government devised a program called Payment in Kind (PIK). You had to figure your cost and bid a number between one and twenty-two. If you were too high, you would receive nothing.

I prayed about what to bid and heard the Lord say, "Twenty-one." But I decided to ask my brother-in-law, who said, "Larry, you cannot bid over eleven." Since he had graduated from Iowa State University, I believed he should know. I bid eleven.

When the results of the program were made public, it showed that twenty-one was the highest number allowed. Had I forgotten that God was smarter than my brother-in-law? That

He was always trying to help me? That disobedience cost me over $10,000. But I was learning to trust His voice and obey.

> "If you are willing and obedient,
> You shall eat the good of the land;
> But if you refuse and rebel,
> you shall be devoured by the sword";
> For the mouth of the LORD has spoken.
> (Isaiah 1:19–20)

A Check in My Spirit

It is a fact that God speaks to us in different ways, perhaps through a still small voice or a prompting from within. He also uses natural things. For example, a red stoplight means stop, green means go, and yellow means use caution. God also uses a check mark, as a teacher marks on a paper. You have probably heard the saying, *a check in my spirit*. This is God's way of loving us because He wants to help us along our way. I'd like to say that I always listened and obeyed, but unfortunately, that is not the case.

It was the Fourth of July, 1975. Our family had not had a vacation in years. We also didn't go far from home for any event due to the livestock chores. My brother Don and his family, who lived about two hours away, had invited us to celebrate the Fourth of July. We all wanted to go, especially my wife and kids. But I had *a check in my spirit*.

It was a sweltering day, and my sows were about to farrow. They were huge, weighing about five hundred pounds, and needed constant attention. My routine was to spray them with cool water three to four times a day to keep their temperatures down.

I had three young men working part time for me. They all assured me that I needed a vacation and that they would take care of everything. My family really wanted to go, and even though I still felt a check in my spirit, I ignored it. We left for Estherville, Iowa. We had been there for only a couple of hours when I felt another urgency in my spirit to return home. Again, I ignored it, convincing myself that the boys would take care of everything.

We arrived back home about eleven that night. The first thing I did was to go to the farrowing house. As soon as I opened the door, a wave of heat engulfed me. Three sows were already dead, and many others were having difficulty breathing. I spent the next few hours trying to cool the remaining sows, but most never fully recuperated. The next day, my son Larry Jr. helped me drag those five hundred-pound carcasses out of the farrowing crates and prep for the rendering works truck. It was a horrifying job and a tremendous financial loss.

The teenage help had begun drinking with their friends and forgot their promises to me. In those days, there were no cell phones to keep in touch. But God had kept in touch with me and tried to alert me, more than once. From my disobedience, I learned several valuable lessons.

- Don't just hear His voice. Obey His voice.
- God always knows best, even if it includes a sacrifice in our eyes.
- Trust God over the voices of people.
- Learn from your mistakes.
- Forgive others and forgive yourself.

Hear instruction and be wise,
And do not disdain it.

Blessed is the man who listens to me,
Watching daily at my gates,
Waiting at the posts of my doors.
(Proverbs 8:33–34)

Who's to Blame?
Although I had learned my lessons, I was still angry at losing
the PIK bid. I was angry at my brother-in-law for not telling
me that he himself decided to change his bid and had submitted one much higher.

"Oh, Larry, I forgot," he said.

I was also angry at the two teenage guys who said they
would look after my hogs while my family and I were gone
and then promptly forgot. It didn't help that it took a week to
clean up the dead hog mess, and money was draining from my
pocket. At my wit's end, I went out to the barn and literally
banged my head against the wall. I had no words.

In His gentle way, God began to minister to my heart.
"I tried to help you, Larry, but you chose not to listen." It
wasn't my brother-in-law's fault or the two young guys who
forgot to tend my hogs. It was my fault. I heard but did not
obey. I asked God for His forgiveness and immediately felt
His peace and comfort. He began to heal my heart.

If you, God, kept records on wrongdoings, who
would stand a chance? As it turns out, forgiveness
is your habit and that's why you're worshiped. I pray
to God—my life a prayer—and wait for what he'll
say and do. My life is on the line before God, my
Lord, waiting and watching till morning, waiting,
and watching till morning. (Psalm 130:3–6 MSG)

CHAPTER 5

Learning to Listen

Trust in the Lord with all your heart, and lean not on your own understanding; in all your ways acknowledge Him, and He shall direct your paths.

Proverbs 3:5–6

"Trust and obey, for there's no other way" are familiar words found in the timeless hymn "Trust and Obey," written by John Sammis (1887). Applying this profound truth has literally saved lives and helped bring souls into the kingdom. Stay tuned to His voice!

Harvest time ended, and it was time to disk down the corn stalks. I was sitting in the cab of my 1466 International tractor with the disk hooked and ready to go. I'd revved up the engine and was just ready to let up on the clutch when I heard the Lord say, "Stop."

With my leg frozen on the clutch, I looked down. My little son was standing in front of the large dual wheels of the tractor. If I had not heard and obeyed His voice, I would have run over my own son. Today, that little boy, Jared, is a grown man serving the Lord and raising a family of his own.

He who is mighty has done great things for me,
and holy is His name.
And His mercy is on those who fear Him
From generation to generation. (Luke 1:49–50)

What Hit Me?

It was clean up day. Granted, it was not a fun job to work through our groves, picking up broken limbs and brush downed by winter's ice and snow. But it had to be done. My kids usually helped as well as a few hired men.

"Dad, I'm sick," Angie, my young daughter, said as we were getting ready to leave. She was still in her pajamas, lying on the sofa. She didn't look sick to me, but something (Someone?) prompted me to let it go.

"OK, Angie, you can stay home," I said, and we left.

The three of us slid in on the bench seat of our new 1974 Silverado pickup and headed for the Wilson farm. If there were more passengers, they had no choice but to sit in the back in the pickup bed. Though seatbelts were mandated by federal law in 1968, they were not enforced in Iowa until the mid-eighties. Passenger safety was not at the forefront of our minds.

We'd had a very productive day, and about five in the evening, we started back. As usual, I had the pedal to the metal, anxious to get home. Suddenly, just ahead I saw a flat-bed truck loaded with sod about to run his stop sign. I didn't have a stop sign and hadn't planned to stop. All I heard was a voice that said, "Turn right." I immediately swerved to the right and felt the impact on my driver's door.

The sod from the flatbed truck completely unloaded into the back of our pickup. Instantly, the image of my daughter Angie lying safely on the sofa at home flashed through my mind. Had I pushed her to go, she would have been riding in the back of the truck. God knew and spared my baby girl. Words cannot express my gratefulness for His prompting again.

> I will praise You, O Lord, with my whole heart;
> I will tell of all Your marvelous works. (Psalm 9:1)

Kaboom!

Another example of God's protection was when Lyn Peed, one of the teenagers who regularly helped me, had returned from chopping cornstalks. It happened so fast. He was refueling the tractor when some of the gas overflowed onto the hot manifold. It exploded into flames and propelled him into the machine shed, slamming him up against the far wall. What a blessing that the machine shed doors were open, allowing him to fly freely. He was not hurt at all, though the tractor was a total loss. God had special plans for him. In the years to come, God would open many other kinds of doors for Lyn, taking his faith and witness around the world through multiple farming and business ventures.

> "For I know the plans I have for you," declares the Lord, "plans to prosper you and not to harm you, plans to give you hope and a future." (Jeremiah 29:11 NIV)

No Work on Sunday

The fourth commandment is to remember the Sabbath day and keep it holy. Ever since recommitting my life to the Lord, I had followed this command very closely. It was late Saturday night. As I was pulling the planter into the shed, I thought I heard God say, "Finish planting the field."

My mind said, *That can't be God.* I went into the house and went to bed.

Sunday morning, I woke up, again with the same strong impression that God was saying, "Finish your fields." I was amazed, but the impression only became stronger. Finally, reluctantly, I climbed on the tractor, hitched up the planter, and went to the field. Later my landlord came out and asked me why I was working on Sunday, and I told him I felt God asked me to finish the fields. By late afternoon, the soybeans were in the ground.

That very night, it began to rain. Significantly, it would be one of the wettest springs on record, raining for the next three weeks. God spared me and my landlord the frustration and tension of unplanted fields and financial loss. He truly knows all things.

> Now it happened that He went through the grainfields on the Sabbath; and as they went His disciples began to pluck the heads of grain. And the Pharisees said to Him, "Look, why do they do what is not lawful on the Sabbath?" . . . And He said to them, "The Sabbath was made for man, and not man for the Sabbath. Therefore, the Son of Man is also Lord of the Sabbath." (Mark 2:23–28)

The Bink Story

He was affectionately known to me as my friend Bink. But it wasn't always that way.

Al Binkley lived about two miles from our farm and frequently rode his horse past our place. Unfortunately, he was usually drunk. It was a nice spring day, and Lyn was again helping me repair one of the hog buildings near the road. Bink was galloping by when he spotted us. He whirled his horse around and rode onto our property, yelling at Lyn to "stop working for that slave driver." He yelled several obscenities at me, then redoubled his efforts to get Lyn to quit work, and finally rode off. We stood silent throughout the whole barrage.

A few weeks later the whole scene repeated, only worse. He was riding his horse down the middle of the road when a car came over the hill. To miss him, the driver swerved into the ditch. Bink flew off his horse, ran threateningly toward the car, yelling at the driver that he had nearly killed him.

Afraid that Bink might do something he'd regret, I ran down to the scene and, by God's grace, persuaded him to get back on his horse and go home. My tractor and a log chain easily pulled the car out of the ditch. Thankfully, no one was hurt. The day ended well.

Winter arrived with a vengeance. Snow already filled the roadway ditches, making it extremely difficult to deal with the new storm that had moved through during the night. School was delayed two hours, allowing snowplows to clear the roads and rural families' their lanes. I mounted the snow bucket on my tractor and plowed a wide path to the road so Jean could get to work. Around midmorning, the school bus picked up the kids. It had already been a long day, so I decided to head into our local Twiggs Café for a cup of coffee. As I passed Bink's acreage, I noticed his truck was stuck in the snow and he was trying to dig it out by hand.

I heard God's voice say, "Help him." I didn't want to deal with his unpredictable behaviors so kept on driving. However, the impression only grew stronger. Reluctantly, I turned around and stopped at the end of his lane. "Hey, Bink," I shouted, "the snow bucket is already on my tractor. Could I scoop you out?"

He was speechless. He lowered his head and with a strained, almost inaudible voice, he answered, "You'd do that for me?"

"No problem. Put the shovel down," I shouted. "I'll be back soon." I gave him a friendly wave and left to get my tractor. Within the hour, his lane was cleared, and his truck was back on the road.

That day changed everything. A few months later, God allowed me to lead him in a prayer of salvation, and Bink's life completely changed.

I learned so many things through my times with Bink. Many of us had been praying over the years for his salvation, including his son Bruce. And God was faithful to answer those prayers. But He continues to bring me back to that day when a small act of kindness literally removed not only the snow from the lane but the snow of his heart. God's love melted years of icy resistance and brought a wanderer into His fold.

> What do you think? If a man has a hundred sheep, and one of them goes astray, does he not leave the ninety-nine and go to the mountains to seek the one that is straying? And if he should find it, assuredly, I say to you, he rejoices more over that sheep than over the ninety-nine that did not go astray. Even so it is not the will of your Father who is in heaven that one of these little ones should perish. (Matthew 18:12–14)

> And let us not grow weary while doing good, for in due season we shall reap if we do not lose heart. (Galatians 6:9)

CHAPTER 6

Good Neighbors

*How good and pleasant it is when God's
people live together in unity!*

Psalm 133:1 NIV

> The power of a united church community has been evident
> in every season of our lives and is the foundational plat-
> form for God's goodness in the world.

You never know what life will bring, and there are times
that we find ourselves in need of help. What a blessing
when that help arrives.

It was springtime 1972, and the usual flurry of field work
was underway, but I was still confined to total bedrest. Two
months earlier, several muscles had torn in my back, and the
chiropractor told me prolonged bedrest was the only cure. He
said I needed to lie flat for three months. After two months,
I felt great. So with fieldwork needing to be done, I went back
to work. In a short time, the tractor hit a rut, and my back had
flashes of such severe pain that I could barely get back to the
house. When I went to the chiropractor again, he said, "Now,
Larry, we start over; lie flat for three more months."

I was so stressed, wondering how I would get all the
spring planting done.

God heard the cries of my heart and literally sent an army. My neighbors organized a huge planting party. Many friends came with their tractors and planters and planted over five hundred acres for us—free of charge. It's impossible to put into words the gratitude we felt as a family toward each of them. God put our hearts at peace.

Several years later, this act of kindness was repeated when another health issue prevented me from riding a tractor. This time it was during the fall season. Again, my farm friends arrived with their combines. What a beautiful sight to see these big machines running side by side bringing in the harvest. Once again, God took care of us. When we had no power of our own, He came to the rescue.

> Are not five sparrows sold for two copper coins? And not one of them is forgotten before God. But the very hairs of your head are all numbered. Do not fear therefore; you are of more value than many sparrows. (Luke 12:6–7)

> And my God shall supply all your need according to His riches in glory by Christ Jesus. (Philippians 4:19)

Our neighbors showed us the power of teamwork and what can be accomplished when working together. Later, when God called us into missions, we saw this principle repeated many times. Multiple teams collaborated with us to alleviate suffering, educate, and provide help to people all over the world. God does not forget what you do for Him.

> And whoever gives one of these little ones only a cup of cold water in the name of a disciple, assuredly,

I say to you, he shall by no means lose his reward. (Matthew 10:42)

Behind the Barn

At the same time, God was drawing me closer to Himself. I was working behind the barn scooping manure when I heard God speak. "Larry, you're straddling the fence. Get on one side or the other, or I will rip you right up the middle." Though I had accepted the Lord as my Savior, I was not really serving Him. I fell to my knees and asked Jesus to forgive me. I began speaking in tongues, and God completely delivered me from smoking, drinking, and swearing. I felt as if a ton of bricks had been lifted from my back. My life was radically transformed. I could not get enough of God.

The afternoon sun came streaming through our living room window as I lay before Him in prayer. He would often nail me to the floor, and I would remain in His presence until He released me. Though I was not a fast reader, I began reading the Bible cover to cover, again and again. That's when God said, "You should start a Bible study." I was very reluctant because I was not a good reader. But He said, "You don't have to read; let others do it."

With that, I visited our pastor and asked what he thought about me leading a Monday night Bible study. He gave his blessing and included it as an activity each week in the Sunday bulletins. Through several pastor changes, the Monday night Bible study remained constant. Eventually, it was handed off to others. At this writing, Dan and Colleen Goodwin are heading the weekly Bible study for friends of the United Methodist Church (UMC) and Somers community. The word goes on.

Don't Forget

A few years after my barn encounter, I borrowed our neighbor's car (for what reason, I can't remember). On the dash lay an open pack of Marlboro cigarettes. I thought, *Why not? One can't hurt.* I lit up and took a puff. Immediately, I heard His voice. "Have you forgotten? I delivered you from all that. Take another puff, and you will be hooked." Immediately, I threw it out the window. *Forgive me, Lord,* I prayed.

> So, since we're out from under the old tyranny, does that mean we can live any old way we want? Since we're free in the freedom of God, can we do anything that comes to mind? Hardly. You know well enough from your own experience that there are some acts of so-called freedom that destroy freedom. Offer yourselves to sin, for instance, and it's your last free act. But offer yourselves to the ways of God and the freedom never quits. All your lives you've let sin tell you what to do. But thank God you've started listening to a new master, one whose commands set you free to live openly in his freedom. (Romans 6:15–18 MSG)

CHAPTER 7

Foundational Milestones

*An important event in the development or
history of something or in someone's life*

"Milestone," Cambridge Dictionary

> The old Lincoln Highway runs through Iowa, and as a boy
> I often noted the "L" cement markers placed along the
> route as we traveled to our grandmother's house. I later
> learned over two thousand markers were erected along
> the highway, beginning in New York state and ending in
> California, commemorating the first coast-to-coast high-
> way in US history. Our lives also have markers—those
> milestones that shape and guide our journey. We are so
> grateful for the foundations laid for us. Building upon
> those foundations remains a lifelong mission.

Jean's great-grandfather was one of the founders of Somers
United Methodist Church; many of her relatives had
attended for generations. We continued that history. Jean
started playing the Hammond organ for Sunday services,
funerals, and weddings when she was fourteen years old. She
received her call to China at a Methodist subdistrict retreat in
Gowrie, Iowa. We were married there, and our children were
all baptized at that altar. We helped with various outreaches,

including sharing our testimonies in different churches as part of the Lay Witness Program. Later Cursillo was introduced. This was a long weekend retreat initiated by the Catholic Church to help people understand and feel the love of God. It was so effective and life changing that Protestant churches adopted it too. We served on a team as often as we could. I had the honor of serving as rector (spiritual head) during one weekend. We were growing in our faith.

Significantly, around 1975, it was also here that Jean and I met our first missionary and witnessed God's provision. It was rare to have a guest speaker, so the pews were packed. As it turned out, she was a single middle-aged lady traveling alone to raise her support. After speaking passionately for about an hour, it was offering time. I will never forget it. As a trustee, it was my job (along with some others) to count the money. What initially seemed promising turned out to be one dollar bill on top of another with a sprinkling of fives and a couple of tens. And then on the bottom of the plate was a folded check. I had to look twice. It was for seventy-five dollars, from a lady with five children and a husband who worked by the hour at a dry-cleaning shop. She literally gave like the widow recorded in Luke 21:1–4. I saw with my own eyes that God supplies all that is needed, though sometimes in unexpected ways.

Side note: For some of you readers who may be thinking this lady acted rashly, ignoring the needs of her family, rest assured. Vy Bates was a lady of faith, integrity, and deeds. God never let her down; He provided, sometimes miraculously, for all her needs too. At age 70, she flew to Albania to help us with the work in Tirane, fulfilling a longtime desire to serve as a missionary. Only God.

And my God shall supply all your need according to
His riches in glory by Christ Jesus. (Philippians 4:19)

Big Heart—Small Sense

I joined the local Prison Fellowship ministry and began serving on teams inside the Iowa State Penitentiary. I must admit,
the sound of iron gates slamming shut was a little unnerving.
Ministry began only after the entire team was searched and
securely locked in with the prisoners. Since the programs
were completely volunteer, we were amazed at how many men
showed up. The Holy Spirit showed up too, and the days flew
by with music, testimonies, and Bible messages. God was at
work in all our hearts. It was a great time, and I made a new
friend. His name was Charlie.

One of the rules for prison ministry was that you never
asked an inmate what he had done. I abided by the rules, so
when Charlie asked if we could keep in touch, I did not give
it a second thought. He seemed like a nice guy. After a few
months, he was released from prison and called to see if he
and his wife could visit us for the weekend. Why not? We
thought it would be great to meet his wife too.

Our kids talk about that weekend even to this day.
Charlie was extremely playful (or reckless) and asked if we
could go outside and play in the snow. We weren't out long
when he picked up our daughter and threw her like a football into a snowbank. We quickly moved the activities back
inside. We decided to play spoons. What could go wrong
with spoons? Charlie became so excited trying to grab his
spoon that he broke his chair, made of solid oak. Not wanting
to miss a play, he picked up the two pieces and tossed them
across the room. We ended up watching TV.

Charlie's wife was a nice lady but also had very memorable characteristics. She had six fingers and six toes, which she delightedly showed our kids. Their eyes were as wide as saucers. The weekend finally ended without further incident. After they left, we tried to explain to our kids that different families have different ways of interacting. We had no idea how true that statement was.

Several months went by. One morning, we received a phone call from Charlie's wife. She was distraught. "Charlie's back in prison," she said. "He started it again. I had to call the police."

"What did he do?" Larry asked. We were not prepared for her answer. "He's molesting our boys again," she answered. We were nearly speechless. Our minds flashed back to the weekend they spent with us. We thanked God for His protection and grace for our kids and us.

But we didn't want to give up on Charlie. We continued to stay in touch, even visiting them once after he was released the second time. Our hearts wanted Charlie to remember that Jesus is ready to forgive and deliver us from any sin. We wish we could report a glorious ending to this story, but unfortunately, Charlie went back to prison, and his family dropped communication. Only God knows. But one thing we do know: if there is breath, there is opportunity for repentance and salvation.

> When Jesus heard it, He said to them, "Those who are well have no need of a physician, but those who are sick. I did not come to call the righteous, but sinners, to repentance." (Mark 2:17)

Big Changes

Farmers are optimists. "It's got to be better next year," I told Jean. We loved our farm life and didn't want to believe the facts that were right in front of us. We had expanded the operation, investing a lot of capital in buildings and hogs. But then came the 1980s. Interest rates rose rapidly. One large farm note was tacked with 21 percent interest, and financially, things began to spiral downward. We sold unnecessary machinery, mortgaged the farm, obtained a supplementary business, and Jean worked full-time in nursing. Our proverbial thinking that everything would be better next year was wrong.

We needed to step away from farming and concentrate on debt reduction. We owed a staggering amount: $480,000. A lawyer in Carroll, Iowa, had been recommended to us as one who could help restructure finances.

He studied our papers for less than five minutes and then said, "You have to claim bankruptcy; there's no other way." When I told him I would not do that, he slammed our folder shut, stood up, called me some unprintable names, and told us to leave. And he charged more than he originally quoted. It was not a happy meeting.

Of course, bankruptcy would bring financial freedom to me but leave the local elevator and other businesses with my debt. My heart could not go there. Yes, it wasn't all my fault with interest up to 21 percent, but I had made the decision to build a hog confinement building and buy bigger machinery. Borrowing was easy; paying it all back was a different story. Once again, I cried out to God, and did He answer! The micro stories below show His extreme grace in helping us erase that debt. Help came from the government, family, friends, and the body of Christ.

One of my landlords, Floyd Wilson, had a precious daughter, Rachael, who suffered severe childhood diabetes. She died at twenty-one. Shortly after her death, Floyd said he'd like to loan the money from Rachael's life insurance policy to us at 6 percent. It was just the amount needed to pay off that glaring 21 percent note.

One of the most painful decisions of my life was to sell the family farm. Dad paid for the 120 acres while raising eight kids. He had sacrificed so much and then sold it to me on contract at 3 percent interest. When farming spiraled down, Production Credit Association (PCA) insisted on it for collateral. I'll never forget the day I had to tell Dad, "I have to sell the farm." His reaction was sympathetic. He told us about how his dad had lost his farm too, in the Great Depression. We didn't deserve the kindness we received, but it showed us a pattern to follow. What a precious father.

Even though things seemed lost, a silver lining began to brighten. I was easily able to sell the farm. In fact, my neighbor, Mike Reed, paid me more than I was asking. I could fully repay Dad. And that interest rate that was so fatal to me was a blessing to Mom and Dad. They earned unprecedented high rates on their savings, helping them live comfortably for many more years.

We had already sold the farm's acreage on a ten-year contract to a local family. They faithfully made the payments, but we needed the full chunk to apply to our debts. One morning in prayer, God said, "Ask Russ and Gayle Sandburg to buy the contract." I was surprised, reluctant, and a bit intimidated, so I put the idea on the shelf. A few weeks later, God reminded me again. This time, though still reluctant, I drove to their home and presented my (God's) idea.

They asked only one question: "Why did you come to us?"

I answered, "God said to."

"That's good enough for us," they responded and bought the contract. Within a month, our debt was substantially reduced again.

Tony Feldman, our accountant, read about a window of financial aid opened by the US government for distressed farmers. Though the time frame had already passed, he made a special appeal. We were gifted $28,000 by the US government.

Jean's grandpa, AW, had loaned us $10,000; he forgave the entire loan.

Federal Housing Association (FHA) also greatly reduced the loan I needed to pay back. And there was more.

Farnhamville, Iowa, was my hometown. With a population just over four hundred, I knew everyone. I sold my hogs to the local stockyards, bought hog feed from the co-op, gas from my cousin Alex who owned the Phillips 66 station, groceries from Freel's, and subscribed to the *Farnhamville Index*, a weekly paper. The big news in town that week was that Judy wanted to sell her recycling business. This seemed like the perfect opportunity to increase my cash flow, and the banker agreed. I became the new owner-operator of Farnhamville Redemption Center. Though it was extremely hard work, it paid off. Each week I picked up 50,000 cans and bottles from grocery and convenience stores and local bars. They were sorted out and sold back to the bottlers. We couldn't keep up and began storing overflow cans in our barn. I didn't know if I could ever get them all sorted out. But unexpected help was on the way.

Who Does That?

Larry Rhoton—that's who. He and I were serving together as elders at New Covenant Christian Church (NCCC). He was a precious brother who knew of our financial situation and had prayed with us for a miracle; however, it did not stop with that. Knowing my barn was full of unsorted cans and bottles, he took much of his free time to help sort my recyclables. It was a dirty and cold job, not anywhere near OSHA standards, but he continued to volunteer until it was done. Everything was sold back to the companies at a penny profit per can. The finished "barn project" netted us $40,000 dollars. Proverbs 18:24 says a real friend sticks closer than a brother. Larry Rhoton was that friend.

But that was not all.

He worked as area manager for a large agricultural company and was transferring out of Iowa to Kansas. He had purchased a fourplex apartment in Fort Dodge and wanted to sell it before leaving. He said to me, "Larry, this apartment really cash flows well. I think it can help you. Round up a thousand dollars, and I'll sign the contract over to you." We were amazed and grateful for his generosity. He exemplified the Scripture in 1 John 3:16–18 (NCV):

> This is how we know what real love is: Jesus gave his life for us. So we should give our lives for our brothers and sisters. Suppose someone has enough to live and see a brother or sister in need, but does not help. Then God's love is not living in that person. My children, we should love people not only with words and talk, but by our actions and true caring.

It took nearly eight years, but we were able to pay back all $480,000. It was a huge relief and a new start. God was beginning a new chapter in our lives—or maybe a whole new book. But let's not get ahead of ourselves. Jean has a story too.

The Formative Years

CHAPTER 8

My Mother, Norma Joan Twigg Moeller

A mother's hug lasts long after she lets go.

—Unknown

> The role of a mother can never be understated. Our stories may be ordinary or not, but one thing is sure: the actions, love, and dedication of our mothers gifted us with an everlasting hug.

I love holding and looking at that black-and-white picture of my mom standing in front of a sprawling pine tree on the Somers Consolidated School grounds. She's smiling happily in her shiny satin majorette uniform, baton in hand. She was a natural choice for drum majorette. Music was in her veins. She'd been tap dancing since she was small.

Her parents, my grandparents, Harry and Agnes Twigg, had owned a successful restaurant and bar called the Coffee Pot in Fort Dodge, Iowa. Mom said she wasn't sure how it started, but around age five, she was tap dancing in the restaurant, imitating Shirley Temple, the child star of the day. Not everyone could see her, so someone suggested she use the bar as her stage. Customers began throwing nickels and dimes at her feet; an innocent act became the new normal. However, a few years later, her parents decided a change was needed. They sold the Coffee Pot, including the recipe for Grandma's famous goon legs (based on the *Popeye* cartoon) and moved to Somers, opening Twigg's Café. Serving coffee and lunches for the farmers was the new norm.

My Father, Little Buddy

Before I share more about my mother, let me introduce my father, Arthur Gilbert Moeller. He was born and raised on the family farm homesteaded by his grandparents in 1879. Before he was old enough for school, tragedy struck; his young mother died of pneumonia. Finding a housekeeper willing to shoulder the responsibilities of four children was daunting. The duties included cleaning a two-story, six-bedroom house, cooking three meals a day for eight to ten people (which might include killing and plucking the chicken), washing all those dishes, laundering clothes in a wringer washer, hanging them outside to dry, hauling them back in, and ironing. All this certainly left no energy for mothering someone else's child. (It almost leaves me breathless to write this!)

Thank God, my dad had his older sister, Mary Eileen, who tried her best to nurture him, calling him Little Buddy. That nickname, Bud, remained with him all his life. Dad never liked it; I think it reminded him of unhappy times. Aunt Eileen (Statler) continued to mother Dad until she moved to Iowa City for university studies. Though Dad was lonely without her, someone else was soon to fill that void.

That fall, my mom entered Somers High School as a new student. She soon caught the eye of my father, Arthur Gilbert Moeller. In 1944, hope became more than a flicker in the hearts around the world. The invasion of Normandy successfully liberated Western Europe from Nazi Germany's control. Big changes were coming for the world. However, in our little bubble in Somers, Iowa, another big change had already begun.

A Little Family History

It was Thanksgiving time when my mom, age seventeen, realized she was pregnant. Expulsion from high school was inevitable. There were no pregnancy crisis centers or helps for single moms, but she didn't need it. My dad quickly took steps to become Catholic so they could be married with the church's blessing. On January 4, 1945, my parents tied the knot, and on July 8, 1945, I was born. It's as if I was born into the arms of God's love. I was premature, weighing in at four pounds, four ounces, and my nose was severely plastered against my face. Mom told me the Mercy Hospital nuns took turns holding me and pushing my nose back into proper alignment. I'm sure they also prayed for me. My faith course was being set.

Within three years, minus one day, my parents had two more kids, Art III and Margaret. Mom was swamped and not even yet twenty years old. More siblings came later: Karl, Brian, and after I was married, Brenda. A definite routine was followed. Each morning, my father's clothes were laid out, milk poured after he sat down at the table because he liked it very cold, and our schedules reviewed on the Farmer's Co-op calendar hanging on the wall. Before I was four years old, I was on the calendar too, scheduled for piano lessons with Miss Miller (at which, initially, I did poorly). Our day ended in front of the refrigerator for our daily dose of Homocebrin (a 1950 liquid vitamin) and cod liver oil.

Dad frequently told Mom how much he loved her and often kissed her in front of us kids. That's why I was so startled to witness a verbal fight. I started crying and yelled, "Does this mean you are getting divorced?"

They both turned and looked at me with expressions that said, *Have you lost your mind?* I never witnessed another altercation.

Before I entered kindergarten, our family made a significant, life-altering change. Mom agreed to attend the local Methodist church where my dad had grown up. It had been difficult for him to accede to Catholic rituals he did not understand. I immediately loved Sunday school and still remember singing, "Climb, Climb Up Sunshine Mountain." We would squat under the pew and slowly come up with our eyes toward heaven. Our teacher said God was looking at us and we should look to Him too.

Where's the Dog?

Art and I were so excited, but Margie, only two years old, didn't understand all the hype. We had seen the poster about the circus and couldn't wait to see that big elephant in the picture. As soon as we entered the tent, it was if we had stepped into another world. I loved the bright lights and especially the music. Color was everywhere—flags, beautiful horses and their riders, and aerial performers right above us. And yes, we did see a huge—and a bit frightening—elephant. He even did a few tricks like bowing and standing on only two feet, which Dad said was hard for an elephant to do. But then came the next act. I can still hear my mom and dad saying, "Jean Ann, look at the dog."

I kept trying, looking from ring to ring, but could never locate the dog. "Where's the dog?" I asked. "What dog?"

Within a month, my parents were driving me to Omaha, Nebraska, a five-hour trek, to see the nearest child optometrist as no one in Iowa could properly check the eyes of a four-year-old. The appointments were long, lying on a hard sofa, waiting for the eye drops to dilate my eyes, and then countless questions as I peered through multiple lenses. Finally, the exam ended, and later, I received my first pair of glasses in the mail. The lenses were thick and ugly. I hated wearing them. But I could see. My music lessons suddenly improved, and schooling was never a problem.

The treks to Omaha continued for years. I deeply regret how ungrateful and whiny I was. It was a huge expense for Dad and an exhausting drive for Mom, but because of their love and care for me, every appointment was kept. I can relate with King David as he cried out to God,

> Do not remember the sins of my youth, nor my transgressions; according to your mercy remember me, for Your goodness' sake, O Lord. (Psalm 25:7)

A Role Model

Mom continued as the "majorette" of our little band. We could count on her having breakfast ready each morning and greeting us as we came off the school bus in the afternoon. We felt secure and loved. Dad also relied on her to monitor the finances and run to the implement dealers for parts or to the vet for special medicine for the animals. She accompanied him to the Omaha Stockyards to buy cattle, which included shopping for us kids. My favorite cattle-trip gift was a bright red ruffled cowgirl dress.

Some summers also included the care of Dad's relatives who viewed the farm as a holiday retreat and Mom as the manager and maître d'. But what is most amazing (and which can only be viewed in retrospect) was her determination to lovingly serve and support all of us, while her own body physically endured one attack after another.

I was only ten when Mom had her first surgery. Over the next decade and half, we watched as she battled multiple medical problems, primarily stemming from her body's inability to retain calcium. Then, on Homecoming night 1972, Larry, Dad, and I rushed her to our local hospital. She had suffered a massive stroke, a cerebral hemorrhage that left her in a vegetative state for five long years. It would take another book to write about all the medical interventions, donated casseroles, prayer vigils, community support, and the effect on each family member through this ordeal.

Larry and I often meditated on the fragility of life, how a life full of vitality could suddenly become so quiet and still. We were searching for answers, but instead, unexpectedly, God asked a question.

The Question

It was a cold wintry night as we backed out of the parking lot of Ellen's Nursing Home. Larry Jr. and Angie were already half asleep in the backseat. We had just visited Mom again, or perhaps I should say we visited Dad. He was with Mom every night, rain, snow, or shine, by her side even though she remained nearly unresponsive. Our only glimmer of hope was when we mentioned the name of Jesus during prayer or Bible reading. Tears would well in her eyes.

Tonight's visit had seemed routine to me, but my husband was deep in thought, almost somber. Finally, I said, "Larry, why so quiet?"

Without looking at me, he answered, "While I was standing by your mom's bed, God spoke to my heart with a question. He asked, 'If that were you lying there, what could you say you have done for Me?' My answer? Not much, Lord."

Shortly after this encounter, God again spoke to Larry, this time out behind the barn (you read about it earlier). These encounters radically changed both our lives. Every Monday night for the next thirteen years, we led a Bible study under the blessing of our local Methodist church. At times nearly forty people attended and occasionally only one or two. The numbers were not important to us, only that we were faithful to what God had called us to do. This dramatic heartache for our family had become the catalyst in our lives to draw us closer to God.

CHAPTER 9

My Grandparents: Culinary Wonders and Jesus

Children's children are a crown to the aged, and parents are the pride of their children.

Proverbs 17:6 NIV

Grandparents reflect the generational legacy that God intended for families. The privilege of having grandparents on both sides of the family is a rare gift. We cannot understate the role of our grandparents in preparing us for the ministry call on our lives.

From the moment of my birth, I was surrounded by a loving family with grandparents on both sides. They made a huge impact on my life.

On my mother's side were Grandpa and Grandma Twigg. Grandma was a very pretty lady with a disposition to match. She worked with Grandpa in the Somers Café every day, preparing food, stocking shelves, and making the famous Twigg donuts. Before this, they ran the Coffee Pot Café in Fort Dodge, Iowa, where Grandma invented the "goon legs" (named for the famous cartoon character Alice the Goon in E. C. Segar's comic strip *Popeye*), which were skewers of BBQ pork, beef, chicken, and lamb. For my birthday, she would bake me an angel food cake with five-minute boiled frosting—all by hand, of course.

Most of all I admired Grandma's quiet and devout faith in God. At the age of eighty years, she felt sick and called Larry and me to pray for her. Larry read Scripture from James.

> Is anyone among you sick? Let him call for the elders of the church, and let them pray over him, anointing him with oil in the name of the Lord. And the prayer of faith will save the sick, and the Lord will raise him up. And if he has committed sins, he will be forgiven. (James 5:14–15)

Grandma and I were seated together on her living room sofa when she asked Larry, "What sin will keep me out of heaven?"

He replied, "Not asking Jesus for forgiveness and accepting Him into your heart."

She immediately asked for us to pray with her. Tears welled in her eyes as she followed Larry in a prayer to receive Jesus. "I feel such a peace," she whispered.

Larry picked up Grandma's large ornate Catholic Bible from its usual location on her coffee table and turned to the Gospel of John. "Start reading here," he instructed her. "You'll get to know Jesus more."

"I think it would be better if I started from the beginning," she said. And so she did. About one year later, she called us and excitedly testified, "Now I know what I did!" She had just finished reading John 3:3–17 where Jesus told Nicodemus, "You must be born again."

> Jesus answered and said to him, "Most assuredly, I say to you, unless one is born again, he cannot see the kingdom of God."

Nicodemus said to Him, "How can a man be born when he is old? Can he enter a second time into his mother's womb and be born?"

Jesus answered, "Most assuredly, I say to you, unless one is born of water and the Spirit, he cannot enter the kingdom of God. That which is born of the flesh is flesh, and that which is born of the Spirit is spirit. Do not marvel that I said to you, 'You must be born again.' The wind blows where it wishes, and you hear the sound of it, but cannot tell where it comes from and where it goes. So is everyone who is born of the Spirit."

Nicodemus answered and said to Him, "How can these things be?"

Jesus answered and said to him, "Are you the teacher of Israel, and do not know these things? Most assuredly, I say to you, We speak what We know and testify what We have seen, and you do not receive Our witness. If I have told you earthly things and you do not believe, how will you believe if I tell you heavenly things? No one has ascended to heaven but He who came down from heaven, that is, the Son of Man who is in heaven." And as Moses lifted up the serpent in the wilderness, even so must the Son of Man be lifted up, that whoever believes in Him should not perish but have eternal life. For God so loved the world that He gave His only begotten Son, that whoever believes in Him should not perish but have everlasting life. For God did not send His Son into the world to condemn the world, but that the world through Him might be saved."

Grandpa Twigg

I loved my grandpa Harry Twigg. He was the town mayor, a small business owner, and a community leader. It was easy to see where my mom got her optimistic personality and dependable work ethic. For forty years, six days a week, he was up at four thirty in the morning and in the café by five. The fifty-cup coffeepot had to be brewed and ready for the six o'clock crowd of farmers. Grandpa, as mayor, was instrumental in setting up free outdoor summer movies. Rough two-by-twelve planks were arranged in rows with a big screen in front. Because his café was the first in Calhoun County to purchase a soft serve ice cream machine, we could enjoy the movie while licking our curly cones. Each cone cost a mere nickel, and Grandpa let me make my own!

On a personal note, my grandparents were some of the first people to buy a Zenith television set. I can still see myself sitting in front of that small black-and-white screen watching *The Magic Window*. This thirty-minute children's educational program from WOI-TV in Ames, Iowa, was hosted by Betty Lou Varnum. I loved her soothing voice and fun crafts. The program became an American classic, running from 1951–1994.

I loved spending time on my grandparents' acreage. They cultivated a big garden, grew cherry and apple trees, and even raised rabbits. We (and the café patrons) were eating organic foods before we knew the phrase *organically grown*. They were an amazing couple.

Life Can Be Hard: A. W. and Edith

Dad farmed with his father, my grandfather, Arthur Warner "A. W." Moeller. A. W. was the thirteenth and last child of German immigrant parents who homesteaded the place in the 1800s. A. W. was an extremely gifted child, brilliant in math. They had square root bees, and he was the champion "square rooter" of his county, able to calculate square root problems in his head.

Though the youngest, he would take over the farm and increase the operation with farms in Minnesota, South Dakota, and even one in North Dakota. Together with his oldest son, John, they created Moeller Hybrid Seed Corn, which he planted on all his own farms and sold to others.

It seems life should have been ideal, but personal tragedy struck. His wife, my grandmother, Mary Francis Quinlan, died of pneumonia, leaving A. W. with four young children. My father, the baby, was only four years old. With so much to do, Grandpa had no choice but to hire housekeepers. It was the 1930s; the Great Depression had brought tremendously difficult times for nearly everyone. Many were looking for work just to eat and provide a roof over their heads. That's when Edith came into the picture. Her husband had died, and the bank had literally kicked her and her two girls out to the street. She saw Grandpa's ad in the paper and applied for work. She got the job. A few years later, she married A. W. and became my Grandma Edith.

God, Trucks, and Hula Skirts
Grandma Edith and her best friend, Ila Johnson, were a two-lady welcoming committee for our Methodist church. They personally visited any newcomers and took food to the homes of the sick. Grandma Edith loved God and worked tirelessly in and out of the home. I once asked her if she ever took a nap, and she replied, "Life is too short to be napping." Her favorite song was "What a Friend We Have in Jesus." We sang it often while she drove A. W.'s truck (without power steering) loaded with seed corn to the sorters in Perry, Iowa.

Grandma also related some of her life stories during our trucking journeys. "You would have laughed," she smilingly said, "if you could have seen me running back and forth with buckets of boiling water, trying to keep that old wringer washer from freezing over." The washer sat outside even in the dead of winter. "I must have looked like a chicken with its head cut off!" She laughed. I'm not sure I could have been so gracious about such a difficult and backbreaking job. But her cheerful optimism rubbed off.

In the 1950s, A. W. and Grandma Edith decided to take a trip of a lifetime and flew Trans World Airlines (TWA) to Honolulu, Hawaii. Few people flew anywhere in those days, so I was a bit worried if they would come back. One month later, they safely returned home, bringing an array of beautiful driftwood items, including a coffee table and gorgeous lamps. But Grandma did not forget me or her other granddaughters. She bought each one of us a real grass hula skirt. We had so much fun pretending to be Hawaiian dancers. I cherished that green skirt for many years.

CHAPTER 10

The Blue Jewelry Box

"For I know the plans I have for you," declares the Lord,
"plans to prosper you and not to harm you, plans to give
you hope and a future. Then you will call on me and come
and pray to me, and I will listen to you. You will seek me
and find me when you seek me with all your heart."

Jeremiah 29:11–13 NIV

I learned early in life that God has the answer to hard questions, difficult situations, and seemingly impossible odds. Our part is to call (pray) to Him, hear Him, and then obey. He has the perfect and unique plan for each one of us. Give Him the reins—let God lead in every season.

Christmas break of my senior year, Larry called to say he'd like to take me to Treloar's Inn, a famous restaurant in Fort Dodge. I was flattered, knowing it was a bit expensive for us. So more carefully than usual, I applied my Mary Kay makeup and dressed up in my new light-green wool pleated skirt and matching angora sweater, popular in the sixties.

Larry seemed extra happy and more relaxed than usual. I thought it was because the pressures of fall harvest were finally over, and he, too, had a winter break. Would I ever be surprised!

As we stepped inside Treloar's, the aroma of barbecue ribs and beans hit our senses. A beautiful all-white artificial Christmas tree (also popular in the sixties) glittered with lights while Christmas music played softly in the background. It was a treat already.

It seems everything is seared into my memory, probably because of the outcome of the evening. I can even remember what I ordered. Larry suggested we share a shrimp cocktail. I said, "They're so small. I'd like my own." A slight look of *Really?* crossed his face. But he graciously ordered two, along with ribs and the trimmings and, of course, our Coca-Cola. The bill was probably a half day's wages. After the movies, we drove home.

We had barely pulled in my parents' driveway when Larry reached up and turned on the dome light. With a big smile, he said, "I got you something," and brought up a beautiful blue leather jewelry box from the backseat. Inside was a stunning solitaire diamond ring. I was still staring at the diamond when he asked, "Will you marry me?"

I was speechless. Of course, I had thought about marriage, but so soon? Finally, I croaked out a whisper. "I need to think about it." To this day, it's hard to explain the look on his face— confusion, disappointment, unbelief? After all, we had expressed our love for each other many times. So didn't it mean anything?

Our evening ended abruptly. I said, "Just give me some time," and got out of the car. Larry backed out of the lane, the blue jewelry box and diamond ring sitting on the backseat.

My stomach was in a knot. My mind was shouting, *You are only seventeen. What about your plans for nursing school? Marriage is forever and ever.*

My mom was elated. Both my grandmas loved Larry and were completely on board. But still, I wasn't sure.

Two weeks went by. My indecision was literally making me sick. School was resuming. How could I go back when I couldn't even think straight? I had to hear from God and was determined to walk our snowy gravel roads until I did. In my heart, I kept praying, *God speak to me. I'm listening.* But all I heard was the crunch of snow beneath my feet. However, as I finished the fourth mile around our section of land, I had a vision of a green light, like you see at city intersections. It remained on green; in fact, I can still see it today. I felt God's assurance that marrying Larry was a "Go."

Larry had gone to stay with his sister in northern Iowa to find work through the winter, so I needed to wait until the following weekend to talk with him. This time, I could hardly wait; however, our initial meeting was cool. Larry wasn't sure that I was sure. "How do I know you won't change your mind again?" he asked.

God's green light vision was strong in my heart; I knew I wouldn't change my mind, but Larry had lost confidence in me. It takes time to repair a blow to the heart. Slowly, we began talking and planning. We decided not to marry until after my first year of nursing. Then we'd prepare our first home on the Wilson farm. Everything was in order. But our plans do not always work out. God had different thoughts that would reorder our agenda.

> For as the heavens are higher than the earth,
> So my ways are higher than your ways,
> And my thoughts than your thoughts. (Isaiah 55:9)

I graduated as planned from Cedar Valley and looked forward to nursing school. Then that letter came in the mail. The nursing program was delayed an entire year because they could not find enough qualified teachers. That I was disappointed is an understatement. After the shock wore off, Larry and I both agreed we were tired of dating and should turn our plans around. Marry first, school second. And so we did. The next six months were a flurry of excitement and planning.

Thank You, Mrs. Fish

My high school home economics teacher, Mrs. Fish, was a self-professed southern belle with very proper ideas for a would-be bride. For years, I kept the nearly three-inch-thick report of fine dishes and silverware patterns we were required to research. She told us, "No respectable girl marries before she has picked out her china and silverware." I learned much about Wedgewood, Lennox, Noritake, and Mikasa place settings; Towle, Oneida, and Rogers Brothers silverware; and of course, daily use brands too. Melmac was a sixties household favorite because it didn't break. (However, a few years later, we found it didn't do well in the microwave.) I also researched furniture styles and home decor.

Wedding plans and preparation of our home on the Wilson farm kept us busy. As mentioned earlier, my mom and grandmas both loved Larry. The wedding planning was a family affair. My wedding and bridesmaid dresses were handmade by a lady in Callender, my mom's friend. The cake was baked and exquisitely decorated by Grandma Edith and our neighbor, Ila Johnson. And Grandma and Grandpa Twigg bought us an eight-piece silver-plated flatware setting as a wedding present.

Larry and I took care of getting our new home ready, red wallpaper and all. When we started to plan our first home, I retrieved my home economics research reports.

Married Years

JEAN

CHAPTER 11

And Then the Honeymoon

*Therefore a man shall leave his father and mother and
be joined to his wife, and they shall become one flesh.*

Genesis 2:24 NKJV

God initiated marriage. Being joined together under God
were not empty words for us. Trials and temptations come.
But as our granddaughter Hayley wrote in magnetic letters
on her dad's refrigerator, "Just Say No," we are reminded
that self-disciple is part of life. Every "no" to Satan's
suggestions brought us closer to each other and Him.

On November 30, 1963, we walked down the Somers
Methodist Church aisle. It was a wonderful day with
three sets of grandparents in attendance as well as nearly 150
family members and friends. Our pastor, Reverend Cyril
Ashton, officiated. His wife, a lady who also had a pastor's
heart, embroidered a beautiful dining room tablecloth, which
we used for over twenty-five years. It was an unforgettable
day of love, celebration, and support.

Honeymoon Nightmare
We decided to honeymoon in Chicago, Illinois. Even though
Larry had never been out of the state of Iowa, and I had only

been on a few Midwest vacations with my parents, we thought it would be an exciting destination. We had no idea.

We left Sunday morning for Chicago, navigating only with Larry's sense of direction. It was already dark when we saw the Chicago skyline illuminated in front of us. We could hardly wait to spend our first night in the big city. We excitedly stopped at the first hotel, then the second and third, all full. Our enthusiasm was ebbing away when finally, we spotted the Blue Light Hotel. The name should have been our clue, but we were desperate. The manager took us up to his "last" room. We had never seen anything like it. All the furniture was painted gray, and you had to walk up to go to the toilet. To flush, you pulled a chain on the wall. But the worst was yet to come.

We hadn't been in bed for more than ten minutes when someone started hammering on our door, yelling, "Let me in! Who's in my bed?"

We both froze. Then we heard the manager say, "Now, Charlie, come with me."

After they left, we pushed the dresser in front of the door and piled a chair on top of that. We lay like toothpicks (we were shaped more like toothpicks in those days) in "his" bed the rest of the night. The next morning the manager asked us if we would like to book another night. We politely said no thank you and rushed out. This "luxury" room was $50, an unbelievable price in 1963.

After this, we thought we should get an overview of Chicago. Taking the Chicago "L" (elevated train) to see the city from above seemed like a good idea. We were really enjoying ourselves until it dawned on us that we didn't remember the station name where our car was parked. A few hours later, we finally got off at the right place. At least our hotel that night was much better and twenty dollars cheaper.

The next day, we planned to go to the Museum of Science and Industry. We got directions from our hotel concierge and started off. We finally arrived but didn't think the building looked like a museum. We had circled the area several times, trying to decide what to do, when finally, a police squad car stopped us and asked if we needed help. We told him we were looking for the Museum of Science and Industry. The look on his face was total disbelief. He simply pointed at the building we had been circling and said, "You're here." We had been looking for the parking lot and kept missing the underground-parking sign until the policeman pointed it out. Unfortunately, we lost so much time that we unable to see the coal mine exhibit. However, the other exhibits were so impressive that over the years, we revisited many times, eventually seeing the coal mine too.

That night, we saw the amazing Broadway production *How to Succeed in Business without Really Trying.* Shopping at Marshall Field's was also on my agenda, so Larry took me the next morning. We were both surprised to see they had the Johnson family's "official" card game, Rook. With that purchase, we headed back to Iowa. Our sweet little farmhouse never looked so good. We always said that having survived our nightmare honeymoon, we could survive anything. However, a few short months later that naïve assumption would be tested.

Wicked Words

> The thief does not come except to steal, and to kill, and to destroy. I have come that they may have life, and that they may have it more abundantly. (John 10:10)

God has great plans for our lives. However, the Enemy (Satan) wants nothing more than to stop those plans and is skillful at using our weaknesses and sinful nature to bring disastrous results. That day was forever seared in my mind, because of my choice to use wicked words. But God . . .

Who started it? What was it about? Who knows. Fights are like that. But I do know that I was determined to "win." Wives know things about their husbands others may not see—they know their vulnerable areas. So at that moment, I decidedly screamed hurtful and damaging words to my husband. To this day, I remember . . . All the color drained from his usual ruddy face, he hung his head, and walked out the door. I was so fixated on myself that I didn't try to make amends. I thought, *Don't worry about him—he'll come back. He always comes back.*

It was midafternoon when Larry walked out. Several hours went by, and he had not returned! It was getting dark. As I looked out the window, I could see that his pickup and our family car were still in the yard. So where could he be? Why hadn't he returned? I began to worry something terrible might have happened and went outside to look. As I approached the machine shed, I was amazed to hear Larry's voice crying out to God: "Lord, help me. What can I do with this woman? Lord, how can I go on?" And then only sobs. Shame and remorse washed over me. How could I have hurt the one I loved so deeply? I ran over to him and pleaded his forgiveness. And in that dark corner of the shed, I pledged to him that I would never use such wicked words or *deliberately* try to hurt him ever again. Larry accepted my apology. And this is our testimony—I kept that promise.

The words of the reckless pierce like swords, but the tongue of the wise brings healing. (Proverbs 12:18 NIV)

Our First Home–Red Wallpaper

Our first home was on the Wilson farm, the same one where Larry played as a boy. It was small by any standards. From the porch, you entered directly into the kitchen. The former pantry was made into a bathroom, and two small bedrooms adjoined the living room. An ugly, black, oil-burning stove, our only source of heat, occupied a good portion of the living room and had to be included in the decor. An Early American theme seemed the answer.

Our local McIntyre Furniture Store in Rockwell City had a great selection of everything we needed. We decided on a high-back sofa and matching chair in brown upholstery with flecks of red, a solid maple console TV, and a nine-by-twelve-foot oval braided rug. I chose an Early American patterned wallpaper in brick red for our kitchen walls, hoping to coordinate the rooms. Larry reluctantly agreed. I had not taken into consideration that this pattern would be difficult to match, especially around three doors and a window. Thank goodness Larry's Uncle Melvin, a professional paint and wallpaper man, helped us. It looked even better on the walls than on the roll and gave a cheery welcome every time we came home.

Our First Dog–Roscoe

About six months after we were married, our good friends, Roger and Donna Brand, said they had a mixed litter of black Lab puppies. "We'd be glad to give you one," Roger said one Sunday morning after church. We could hardly wait. That afternoon we drove to their farm to have a look. When we first saw Roscoe, we were in love. His black eyes seemed to say, *I'm the one*, while his tail wagged as if there were a hundred flies to swat. We took him home.

Roscoe was a family member from the start. Larry had taken a supplemental job in Fort Dodge, which meant I had many lonely hours by myself. One evening I walked out, sat down on the porch step, and again rehearsed my plight of being stuck on a farm while my friends were in college having a wonderful time. It seemed Roscoe could sense my mood. He quietly walked over, put his paw on my leg, and looked at me with *so-sorry* eyes. Hugging him tightly, I said aloud, "You're such a blessing, Roscoe. Thank God for you."

Suddenly, I felt God's Spirit gently reminding me that Roscoe was not my only blessing. The words of an old hymn rose in my heart: "Count your many blessings, name them one by one. Count your many blessings, see what God has done." I started to cry and regretted spending so much time in self-pity when I was surrounded with numerous blessings. I made a new plan. On the evenings when Larry worked, I drove to our church and used that time to practice the music for Sunday's service. Words from the hymns and music of that Hammond organ always lifted my spirit and changed my focus.

Roscoe's sensitivity had helped me readjust my life. But he was especially close to Larry, accompanying him while doing chores or lying quietly beside him while he adjusted field equipment for spring work. He guarded us all with a warning bark whenever someone turned into our lane. And as our young son Larry Jr. grew, Roscoe became his friend too, attentively watching over him as he played in the yard. We often said that Roscoe was our family guardian. And he was about to prove it.

It was late spring, and Roscoe again took up his habit of running to the creek bordering our property for a swim. This spring had been unusually wet, and with the snow melt, the water level was high.

Larry and I had just poured a second cup of coffee when I realized Larry Jr. was not around. It didn't take long to check our small house and discover he wasn't inside. How did he get past us and out the door? How long had it been? Larry immediately ran outside and began checking the farm buildings, hoping and praying he had not gotten into a sow's pen. Thank goodness he wasn't there either. I was rechecking the upstairs of our house, when I heard Larry yelling, "Roscoe, come here boy." He yelled again and again. I ran outside in time to see Roscoe running back across our field with Larry Jr. close behind. We both continued shouting, "Come here boy. Come here, Roscoe," as we ran toward them. A few minutes later, Larry Jr. and Roscoe were in our arms.

We were overwhelmed with God's goodness. Larry had spotted Roscoe and our son near the bank of the creek. Not only did God speak to Larry's heart to stop and call the dog, but He also gave us an obedient dog. As soon as Roscoe heard Larry's voice, he immediately changed directions and came running home, abandoning his routine swim in the creek.

Blessed are all who fear the Lord, who walk in obedience to Him. (Psalm 128:1 NIV)

Roscoe certainly was a big blessing to us, but he was just a foreshadowing of the many blessings to come. Through the years, we've often thought back to that day. Are we willing to immediately change our routine and act on the prompting or voice of the Lord? Should not we be as obedient to God as Roscoe was to us?

Only God.

CHAPTER 12

Nursing Dream Awakens

Then the Lord replied: "Write down the revelation and make it plain on tablets so that a herald may run with it."

Habakkuk 2:2 NIV

> Dreams and visions are what propel us toward a goal. Whether we actually write them down or seal them in our hearts, faith and patience will bring them to pass. Don't give up.

Larry and I were married and already had three children. But I still had that old dream to become a registered nurse. A nursing scholarship was granted to me right out of high school, but the program had been delayed a year because they could not find sufficient accredited teachers. Larry and I decided to marry and begin our business of farming. However, during the 1980s, farming had become a financial disaster. I needed to get a job that would help put us back on our feet. We began praying about it and decided I should go to school for a nursing degree. Of course, this cost money we did not have.

On a blistering July morning, I was pulling weeds by hand from our half-mile soybean rows on the F. Johnson farm. To my surprise, my eighty-year-old grandpa, A. W., was walking toward me. I asked him what he was doing out in the sun. He simply replied, "I needed to see you. I heard you want to go to nursing school. Don't worry about finances, Jean Ann; I'll pay for it all."

I was overwhelmed with God's goodness and asked, "How can I repay you, Grandpa?"

"When you can, help someone else in need."

Though he didn't know the term *pay it forward*, he modeled it with his life. Grandpa later established a scholarship fund through the Somers United Methodist Church to help future medical, agricultural, or pastoral students with their education. He believed in the next generations.

That fall, I entered Fort Dodge Community College's nursing program. At the time, I had no idea how important this would be to us, not only in the immediate future but in the years ahead. Only God!

Preparation Time

God's timing is so amazing. Even before graduation, I was hired to work at Friendship Haven, a large nursing home with an excellent reputation. Beds were filled as fast as they became available from a long waiting list. The campus also included apartments for assisted living.

Grandma Twigg was now over eighty years of age and living alone on her acreage. Because both of her children had died early and now Grandpa, too, it was up to us grandkids to look after her. Because we were worried about her safety, we suggested she move to an assisted living facility. She cried and continued to cry every time we approached the subject. Eventually, I persuaded her to consider a room at Friendship Haven where I worked.

Since Friendship Haven was partially subsidized by the Methodist church, the conference assigned pastors to manage the selling or rental of the apartments and to raise funds for the home. Pastor Vern Sorenson, our friend from Cursillo days, was serving in that position. He met with Grandma and me and showed us a room in the basement. It had only one small window high up on the wall. Grandma burst into tears. I could not hold back my tears either. Pastor clearly felt empathy toward us and suggested we look at another room. It had a large window with a tulip tree (so rare in Iowa) blooming right outside. It was the perfect room for her. When we asked if Grandma's budget would be sufficient, Pastor Vern (who held that position for less than a year) said, "Let me see what I can do." Within the month, Grandma had a new home. God certainly placed him there at just the right time to bless my faithful Grandma.

A short time later, I stopped to visit Grandma in her new room. She started crying again! She told me she was so sorry for putting up such resistance. "I can't thank God enough for bringing me here. It's wonderful," she said. She lived there until God took her home at age ninety-six.

After a few years at Friendship Haven, I switched jobs and worked at Trinity Regional Hospital. I loved working there too. Since it was a thirty-minute drive both ways, we began discussing a move to Fort Dodge. However, Larry told me he would only move if we could live there rent-free. I thought that was ridiculous and we'd never move. But hold that thought; we are not quite there yet.

CHAPTER 13

A Three-Wheeler Builds Faith

But without faith it is impossible to please Him, for he who comes to God must believe that He is, and that He is a rewarder of those who diligently seek Him.

Hebrews 11:6

Step by step, faith builds. It can be exciting and scary at the same time. Whether sitting in front of an Iowa banker praying for a loan or believing God to provide a three-wheeler for a young son, the principle is the same. Do what you can do and then trust the Lord for what you cannot do. As He brought us through many nearly impossible situations, another brick was cemented into our wall of faith.

Life is a step-by-step process. Not only did we faithfully support our Methodist church in attendance and tithing, serving on the board, and leading the Monday night Bible study, but we also increasingly took part in evangelistic opportunities. We joined the Lay Witness team and began speaking in other local churches.

Later, the Methodist Conference introduced the Cursillo weekend. This was a three-day retreat designed to allow people to experience God's love. A team of twenty or more people served the "candidates" in prayer, inspirational talks, and delicious food. The final day simulated our entrance to heaven with a joyous standing ovation from family and friends. We served on the teams as often as possible—Larry as rector (spiritual leader) at one of them. Many lives were miraculously changed. One man, though married for more than ten years, could for the first time tell his wife that he loved her. The renewing, healing work of the Holy Spirit was evident over and over. Larry also took another step, serving as literature officer for our local Full Gospel Businessmen's organization, distributing Christian materials to doctors' offices in multiple cities and speaking at some of the meetings. God had been preparing us for the next step. And it was just around the corner.

One evening, after our Full Gospel Businessmen's meeting, friends invited us to join a new church plant in Fort Dodge. Though the Somers Methodist Church had been our home for so much of our life (mine since nursery days), we felt God initiating a change. The following Sunday we made a visit. As soon as we walked through the doors of New Covenant Christian Center, we knew God had called us to this new work.

But how do you step away from the church, friends, and relatives you love? After much prayer, Larry decided we should write a letter to the pastor and board and ask for their blessing. Their response was to throw a going-away party! After a grand potluck supper (as only Methodist ladies can do), church leaders presented me with a plaque for playing the organ for twenty-five years. We were totally overwhelmed with their outpouring of love. Before the evening ended, we asked if everyone would form a circle for closing prayer. As we held hands, forming a powerful, God-centered circle, Larry prayed, "May this circle never be broken, until we all meet again in heaven. Amen."

Did We Hear You, Lord?

New Covenant Christian Center (NCCC) was established under the pastorate of Dave and Kris Toyne. The praise and worship and preaching instilled in us a new expectancy of God. Our faith blossomed.

Within the year, Pastor Dave appointed Larry as an elder. Shortly after, trouble erupted, and the small congregation split. In all our years at the Methodist church, we had not seen such trouble. And just on the heels of that terrible event, Dave announced he was moving to pastor another church in Clear Lake, Iowa. We didn't know if the church could survive. *Did we hear You, Lord? Were we really supposed to join NCCC?* We did not hear God say to go, so we steadfastly remained.

Pastor Mike and Janis Carmody

They were a young family from the Clear Lake area. Pastor Mike "tried out" one Sunday morning and fell off the old-style Lutheran church pulpit. He was only the second potential pastor who had preached at the church, but Larry Rhoton and my Larry (the remaining elders) felt that he was to be our new pastor. We were so sure that we called him that very afternoon and offered the job. He accepted, and we moved them to Fort Dodge during a snowstorm. Thank goodness, that was not an omen of things to come. On the contrary, they led NCCC faithfully for many years. After we left for the mission field, the church moved to a new location and remains alive and well today under the pastorate of Mike and Janis's son, Joshua, and his wife, Alicia. Praise God.

Are You Kidding?

We loved being part of NCCC and were driving back and forth forty-five miles round trip at least three times each week. And I was making the same trip to work five times a week. We both felt a move to Fort Dodge would be advantageous. However, there was *that* problem. Remember? Larry said he would not move unless he could live there rent-free. I still thought he was kidding, but then he started telling other people the same thing. His words to me? "Have faith!"

Finally, a local realtor contacted us and said she had a vintage home she'd like to show us. As she drove us down Eighth Avenue North, lined with old maple and oak trees, we looked at each other in amazement. We loved trees. But the best was yet to come. The house was a stately brick home built by a Fort Dodge banker in 1913. Everything was exquisite: stainless-steel appliances, dining room chandelier, built-in oak grandfather clock, and a fully renovated basement with walnut paneling. The upstairs floor had been converted to two large apartments with the proper paperwork for legal rentals. We both loved the house and tried to contain our enthusiasm long enough to make a business-minded offer.

We can't say it enough. Only God. The income from those upstairs apartments and the fourplex that Larry Rhoton had transferred to us would more than pay the mortgage. I could see God working through my husband. My faith grew!

A Three-Wheeler Builds Faith

Patience and perseverance to remain on our strict, debt-reducing budget was often more difficult than I initially imagined. Angie needed a new dress for spring prom. I will always remember telling her she could only pick from the sale rack. There wasn't much to choose from, but she finally decided on a yellow taffeta dress with puffed sleeves; much prettier dresses were only a few steps away. Angie, true to herself, didn't complain, but I was crying on the inside. This was not the experience I had imagined for my only daughter.

Angie's date was Clay Sandburg, whom she later married. When relating this story to Clay, he smiled and said, "I wasn't looking at the dress; I was looking at the girl." At this writing, they have been married thirty-one years.

More disappointment seemed inevitable. Christmas was coming. In years past, presents were stacked high around the tree, but now there were no extra funds for nonessentials. We warned our kids that this Christmas would be different. Even so, our ten-year-old son Jared seemed undeterred. His heart was set on a three-wheeler motorbike. Maybe we needed the faith of a little child? Only God could orchestrate the following.

It was mid-December. Jared's Sunday school teacher, Larry Rhoton, finished the "Faith of a Mustard Seed" lesson by asking the class for prayer requests. Jared immediately said, "I want a three-wheeler for Christmas, but my parents don't have money to buy it for me."

Larry's response? "Let's pray." And he asked God to provide a miracle for Jared to build his faith.

> So the Lord said, "If you have faith as a mustard seed, you can say to this mulberry tree, 'Be pulled up by the roots and be planted in the sea,' and it would obey you." (Luke 17:6)

One week before Christmas, Daddy Larry was looking through the ads in our local newspaper when he spotted "For sale or trade, three-wheeler in great condition." He called the number. The seller said the three-wheeler was worth about

$1,600, but he would trade for an old pickup. My husband could hardly believe his ears. We had the exact old pickup truck the seller was looking for. But there was a problem—it didn't run.

"It doesn't matter," the seller said. "I'm replacing the engine anyway." So with Larry Jr.'s help, the pickup was delivered, and the three-wheeler brought home and hidden away till Christmas.

It was a cold, snowy Christmas Eve. After we had unwrapped the gifts under the tree, Daddy Larry said to Jared, "There's one more thing, but we have to go outside to see it." Earlier, Larry Jr. had backed our pickup near the house with the three-wheeler concealed under a tarp. As soon as we were all outside, Larry Jr. hopped into the pickup bed and threw off the tarp, exposing the three-wheeler.

Jared stared as if in shock. Finally, he said, "Hey, Lar, that's a super bike. I hope you like it."

With a big smile, Larry Jr. said, "It's not mine. It's for you, little buddy."

Jared burst into tears. I couldn't hold back my tears either. For a few minutes, before the severe cold forced us back into the house, Angie and I watched the "boys" point out the special features of the bike: Honda 200X, not stock but a souped-up version, probably the fastest in the county. Jared still testifies, "It was a huge faith builder for me. I knew God had heard my prayers." As for Larry and me, our faith was strengthened too.

CHAPTER 14

Living Rent-Free
in Fort Dodge

*Also I heard the voice of the Lord, saying: "Whom shall I send,
And who will go for Us?" Then I said, "Here am I! Send me."*

Isaiah 6:8

Though the call to full-time missions came early in our
lives, it was God who arranged the sending time. Through
nearly a thirty-year wait, He was building faith and sharp-
ening the tools needed for our ministry journey. And what
a journey it is!

We loved serving the church. If the doors were open, we
wanted to be there, to be in the presence of God. It was
a time of spiritual growth. Since we had such a big home, we
had the privilege to host numerous ministries and missionaries visiting the church. We volunteered for everything from
teaching to mowing the grass.

Our family and friends had just left after moving us from
the old farmhouse to this beautiful home in Fort Dodge. We
were standing together in the kitchen. I was babbling on and
on about how much I loved my beautiful new home, the solid
oak molding, built-in grandfather clock, plush light-beige

carpeting, and fully finished basement with real walnut paneling. The red rose furniture the banker's wife had sold us seemed
like a dream to me. When I finally took a breath, Larry quietly
said, "Don't get comfortable. We won't be here long."

I couldn't believe Larry's words. Astounded, I angrily
responded, "Don't tell me that. I'm staying here for the rest
of my life." But in my heart, I knew he was right.

The house served us well for that season of our lives.
I loved city life. My commute to work was about five minutes.
Everything you needed was just a trip to the mall. But for
Larry, it was much different. We never locked a door on the
farm, and it was hard for him to remember his house keys.
However, the pluses for us all far outweighed the drawbacks.
And the best thing? We were close to our church.

Will You Go?
I first heard the call of God the summer of 1961. John F.
Kennedy had become the first Catholic president of the United
States. During his inaugural address, he uttered these famous
words: "Ask not what your country can do for you—rather,
ask what you can do for your country."

I was at a summer retreat for teens in Gowrie, Iowa. The
Methodist district had sent a new, fiery young pastor to preach
our closing session. It was evident he had a passion for souls.
After quoting JFK's iconic words, he fervently challenged us,
"Ask not what God can do for you; rather ask what you can
do for God. Go, sit alone in the woods until you hear what
God wants you to do!"

It was early evening as I obediently left the lodge and
followed the gravel path into the woods. A few minutes later,
I spotted a flat rock and sat down. Half-heartedly, I said out
loud, "OK, God, what do you want me to do?"

In a short time, I audibly heard one word: "China."

I was shocked. China was not on my radar or anyone else's during the early sixties. So I asked again, "Is there anything else, God?" I would hear "China" two more times.

I was so excited to know that God had called me to be a missionary in China. However, my family was not. In fact, my dad would shake his finger at me and declare, "No daughter of mine will ever set foot in China."

Although I buried the dream deep in my heart, I was assured that when God speaks, you can count on it.

It Will Come to Pass at Just the Right Time
Time marched on. My husband and I were now in our mid-forties, living in Fort Dodge. The call of God to do full-time mission work was growing stronger. We had worked on several short-term mission trips with Feed the Children from Oklahoma City. The team opened medical clinics each day in remote areas of Central America and Thailand. While hundreds of people waited to see Dr. Beihler or one of us nurses, Larry walked the lines talking to individuals about Jesus. We were never ready to go home, and when we got home, we were ready to go right back.

Though we sensed God wanted us to step into missions full-time, my main concern was how we would be supported. Our short-term trips were fully paid by the church, but Pastor Mike made it clear that the church would only support a portion of our ministry needs. He said it wasn't healthy for one church to be the sole supporter for a couple of reasons. If the church had a downturn or split, the finances may be cut drastically, crippling our work or taking us off the field entirely. Multiple supporters would ensure increased prayer support and a wider distribution of income.

I had also become complacently comfortable with our position in the church, my well-paying job as a registered nurse, children growing up, and friends. In fact, I was the one now straddling the fence, wanting to go, wanting to stay.

On the other hand, Larry's faith grew stronger. He kept reminding me, "God has seen us through so much. If we continue to listen to His voice, He will also take care of us on the mission field." After our meeting with Chuck and Marge Wyatt (written later in our story), I felt the call had to override my fears. It seemed time to take the next step.

That's when Pastor Mike Carmody showed us the flyer from Victory Christian Center. He also encouraged us: "You will never need to worry about finances. God sees all you have done for the church and others. It's stored in His bank for your use." (Pastor Mike had seen us give away a car, borrow money to give to the church, excuse a widow lady eighteen months rent, and serve in other multiple ways.) Pastor Mike was right. In thirty years of ministry, we have never had lack. Some months were down to the wire, but the next month picked back up. Our main key to ministry finances is, again, hear the voice of God. He never asks you to begin something He is not already prepared to support.

Admittedly, I had been dragging my feet, letting the world crowd out God's call. Though Larry's faith in God's provision never wavered, he was patiently waiting for me to get on board. And God, in His perfect timing, arranged a catalyst meeting with Chuck and Marge Wyatt.

Ministry Years
LARRY AND JEAN

CHAPTER 15

The Call

*I will tell of the kindnesses of the Lord, the deeds for which
he is to be praised, according to all the Lord has done for us.*

Isaiah 63:7 NIV

We were called to go, but it would take a team to complete
the mission God placed in our hearts. Every partnership,
whether in the USA, Albania, China, Africa, Canada, or
other nations, has been by the divine hand of God. He
opened the right doors at just the right time. Our stories
are full of many beautiful and talented people whom He
brought alongside us to further His kingdom. God's timely
intervention is amazing and at times miraculous. Read the
stories. Let faith arise!

We were serving as elders at NCCC and had moved into
our Fort Dodge home with the upstairs apartments.
One was rented by a wonderful couple, Chuck and Marge
Wyatt. We will never forget the evening they invited us out
to dinner at one of Fort Dodge's nicest restaurants.

The waitress had just placed a sizzling ribeye steak in front
of each of us when Marge burst into tears and Chuck looked
like he was about to join her. Finally, they collected themselves
and explained that God had called them to minister at Red

Bird Mission in the Appalachian Mountains of Kentucky. Sorrowfully, they related how they let the circumstances of everyday life dictate their choices. "We refused to go," Marge recounted, "and carry that remorse to this very day." Again and again, they repeated, "Don't miss the call. You will regret it the rest of your life."

Their words confirmed what God was telling us. It was time to go!

> Also I heard the voice of the Lord, saying: "Whom shall I send, and who will go for Us?" Then I said, "Here am I. Send me." (Isaiah 6:8)

As we continued to pray and reflect on our conversation with Chuck and Marge, the call became stronger, more urgent. A short time later, we met with Pastor Mike and asked his counsel on how to proceed as missionaries. He reached into his desk and gave us a pamphlet, saying he believed it was for us. The pamphlet was from Victory World Missions Training Center in Tulsa, Oklahoma.

Larry and I were amazed. Could God be paving the way now for us to answer the call? Since it was already late summer, we decided to make a personal trip to the Victory campus. The director, Todd Powers, felt we were to come. Since the new training began in September, he told us there was not enough time for the paperwork. "Just get here."

Our walk of faith had begun. And as if God were truly giving us the green light, Chuck and Marge gave us our first offering. We would be (and continue to be) amazed at the provision and support that God provided through His people. Every penny we needed, God abundantly supplied.

Sweet Vy

Vy was an amazing lady who had great faith in God. Remember how in 1975, she sacrificially blessed a missionary at the Somers Methodist Church? Fast forward to 1987. Vy, whose husband, Ken, had died several years earlier, followed us to NCCC in Fort Dodge and worked there as the church secretary. She was faithful in all areas, even babysitting our pastor's two small children.

When God called us to full-time missions, finances threatened to be an obstacle—the mission school in Tulsa was not cheap. The Bible says in Jeremiah, "Before you call, I will answer." Certainly, He proved Himself again. Vy stepped up with an offering to cover the entire cost of VWMTC mission school. All her life, she lived frugally but gave extravagantly to the kingdom of God. Now her seeds are blooming all over the world.

> Now Jesus sat opposite the treasury and saw how the people put money into the treasury. And many who were rich put in much. Then one poor widow came and threw in two mites, which make a quadrans. So He called His disciples to Himself and said to them, "Assuredly, I say to you that this poor widow has put in more than all those who have given to the treasury." (Mark 12:41–43)

CHAPTER 16

We Will Go

Go therefore and make disciples of all the nations,
baptizing them in the name of the Father and of the
Son and of the Holy Spirit, teaching them to observe
all things that I have commanded you; and lo, I am
with you always, even to the end of the age. Amen.

Matthew 28:19–20

> The mandate is clear. All men and women need salvation.
> What joy to bring the gospel to many around the world,
> and yet so much more is needed to be done. Will you grab
> the mantle? Will you run the race?

It was time to go! But before Larry and I just took off, we talked with all our kids. Our daughter, Angie, had recently married Clay Sandburg, her boyfriend of almost eight years. They agreed to our faces that we should follow the call of God but several years later confided they had thought we must have been nuts. However, despite their true feelings, in those early years, Clay and Angie decided to be involved with our ministry. Because we had sold our home and apartment house to go on the mission field, we had no place to call our own. The two of them immediately opened their door for a home base. Usually, it is the child who comes home to the parents, but in our case, it was the parents coming home to the children. Today, Angie is the registrar for Will Go Inc. and continues serving in many ways.

Our greatest cheerleader, however, was our youngest son, Jared. God worked through him so that we could and would go. It was his senior year of high school. Jared was well liked, president of his high school band, and active in various clubs and church. So you're asking yourself, *What parent would leave their son at such a time?*

But he assured us "nothing important" was scheduled at school and he could handle the apartment rentals. "Trust me," he said. We packed our bags and left for Tulsa. Only later did we learn that Jared was Master of Ceremonies at a major school program. During our absence, he also had the unpleasant job of evicting a renter, cleaning the place, and re-renting it. He was such a blessing.

Only years later did Jared confess to us, "As you pulled away from the house, it felt like my right arm had been ripped off. I knew you needed to go, but I felt like an orphan. I had to remind myself that I was serving God, too, by helping you guys." God's Word tells us in 1 Peter 5:10 that after we have suffered awhile, God will restore us and make us strong, firm, and steadfast. And God did that for us all. In January 2005, only a few months after Jared and Heather were married, they moved from Chicago to Blaine, Washington, to help us establish Will Go Ministries (Canada).

Their faithful presence was a special gift from God, allowing us to redeem time apart. Later, they moved back to the Chicago area and opened their home to us. God had placed them right on the path to most of our supporting churches. An added blessing was seeing our two grandchildren, Jaden and Hannah.

Our oldest son, Larry Jr., married Alisa in 1993. They had a beautiful baby girl, Hayley Ann Johnson (Ann after Grandma J). When you see and hold such a precious one, it is awfully hard to leave. But as Larry Jr. told us, "We are all on our own, so just do what you think you have to do." His home in Fort Dodge has always been open to us too. We are extremely blessed.

Be a Family

There was only one thing we asked of our children: stay together as a family, always love and forgive each other. It would be heartbreaking to come home and find an angry, fragmented family. Thank God, this request has been practiced to this day. Angie and Clay were the first to step up, hosting almost every Thanksgiving and Christmas family gathering for more than fifteen years. Now everyone takes a turn hosting.

Victory—Tulsa, Oklahoma, 1991

We arrived at Victory World Mission Training Center (VWMTC) to train as missionaries. Little did we know that a difficult high ropes course would be part of the curriculum. Climbing to the top of a telephone pole was extremely challenging for Larry, not only because he had a fear of heights but also had a painful, sprained foot. Getting to the top was not all; you then needed to jump toward a flying trapeze. For me, that part was not as difficult as walking a tightrope some twenty feet in the air. I fell and had to scoot across the wire on my bottom to the other side. It took six months for all the bruising to disappear. However, after completing this two-day challenge, all fear left us. As God gave victory over the obstacles on the course, we knew He would also give us victory over any obstacles on our journey for Him.

The missions training also included a reading assignment of fifteen different books. *From Jerusalem to Irian Jaya* by Ruth Tucker had a profound influence on us. This book consisted of multiple missionary stories. It was not a glorified rendition of triumph and victory—quite the opposite. Story after story recounted the in-fighting of missionaries. Sometimes whole ministries or projects were scrapped because people refused to cooperate and move beyond some perceived offense. After finishing this book, Larry and I prayed that we would not be a stumbling block to the kingdom of God and would, to the best of our ability, keep our flesh under control, as Galatians 5:24 says,

> And those who are Christ's have crucified the flesh with its passions and desires.

CHAPTER 17

Mexico

Heaven and earth will pass away, but
my words will never pass away.

Matthew 24:35 NIV

Mexico—Mexico is the southernmost country in North America, with thirty-one states and a federal district. Like the US, they each have their own laws and police. Sixty-nine different languages are spoken, which necessitated more than one translator when preaching. Mexico is famous for her cathedrals, thirty-four UNESCO sites, oldest North American university (founded in 1551 by Charles V), food, and Mariachi bands. However, our focus was her people—to bring them the liberating and everlasting Gospel of Jesus.

Our missions school training ended with a trip to southern Mexico. We had practiced pantomimes, skits, songs, simple Spanish phrases, and short messages. I was personally looking forward to ministering with Larry and spending time together. My expectations could not have been more wrong. First, Larry was designated to drive the van loaded with supplies all the way to Mexico City. The rest of us flew. Second, we were stunned to learn couples would not be allowed to share a room. Larry was assigned a closet-sized room with another teammate and his unhappy two-year-old son. I and several other ladies shared a dormitory with only one bathroom. But this was just a tiny taste of the challenges to come.

Ministry Time

In the early nineties, Mexico City had a population of sixteen million (today, over twenty-two million). We planted ourselves just outside an exit of the Metro, an underground transit system, and set up our music. The fun pantomimes and effective preaching drew hundreds of people. Many received prayer, and seeds were planted.

Two days later we vanned south, where we met our guides, seasoned trackers in the Sierra Madre de Oaxaca mountain range. We all looked forward to this evangelistic outreach, especially meeting the people. We were not disappointed. Though we were physically exhausted from lack of sleep and the difficult climb, our spirits were renewed at the sight of so many people in colorful clothing surrounding their humble church; the inside was already fully packed. We learned many had even arrived the day before. Expectation was high and the excitement tangible.

Larry was one of the speakers, which included two translators, English to Spanish and Spanish to the local dialect. They were so open and tender before the Lord. Many came forward to receive Jesus in their hearts. Our ministry teams prayed for everyone, including the sick and demonically possessed. Demons forced one wretched lady to slither up the wall like a snake. We continued to lay hands on her, commanding the demons to come out, until eventually she sat quietly on the floor and prayed with us to accept Jesus. My prayer for her was that she would remain free all the days of her life.

When a corrupting spirit is expelled from someone, it drifts along through the desert looking for an oasis, some unsuspecting soul it can bedevil. When it doesn't find anyone, it says, "I'll go back to my old haunt." On return, it finds the person swept and dusted, but vacant. It then runs out and rounds up seven other spirits dirtier than itself and they all move in, whooping it up. That person ends up far worse than if he'd never gotten cleaned up in the first place. (Luke 11:24–26 MSG)

The Meal
The missions team consisted of more than twenty people. The villagers had prepared rice and beans and roasted the village goat, but they had not expected so many big, hungry Americans. They graciously shared all they had. It was a humbling experience as I'm not sure they had much to eat.

Day Two
The plan was to continue farther into the mountains to another church. But during the night, it began to rain and showed no signs of letting up. Should we push on in faith? Just as our mission's director, Todd Powers, was considering our options, a runner came into the village. He said, "Get the Americans back down the mountain. The passes are too slippery. Two runners have already lost their lives from mudslides."

Denunciano, our main guide, simply said in broken English, "Move now."

How Slow Can You Go?
The rain continued and conditions were deteriorating. Everyone had their stick to help keep steady, but we were like

slugs inching down the mountain. Denunciano was becoming more alarmed at our pace and would come up beside us and say, "Move, move." Finally, he took matters into his own hands. He began taking us ladies, one by one, down the mountain at lightning speed. He was shorter than my five-foot, two-inch frame, but he was powerful. He lifted me up under one arm, shouting, "Move feet, move feet!" With my backpack and all, we flew. What would have taken me another two-plus hours, he accomplished in thirty minutes. I tried to keep my feet moving, but they kept banging against the rocks. I lost all my toenails on both feet from that run, but I am not complaining. God certainly provided a deliverer for me. Without Denunciano, I may have lost a lot more. He seemingly never took a break or a breath. He was back up the mountain to bring down one more person, and then one more.

Larry was more than two hours behind me. We had been instructed to pack very lightly; however, one young lady had packed everything but the kitchen sink. She could not move at all in the mud, so Larry included her pack with his. I was really concerned for him. His compassionate heart literally burdened him beyond what even he could or should handle. No one offered to relieve him; it was all they could do to get down themselves. I was never so glad to see his face coming around that last turn. Truly, "I can do all things through Christ who strengthens me" (Philippians 4:13) came to our hearts and minds.

Denunciano

With everyone safely at the foot of the mountain, Denunciano encouraged us to never give up on anyone by sharing his own remarkable transformation in Christ. To say he was sold out to Jesus would be a gross understatement. He lived and breathed to share the gospel and win another one to the kingdom. But it wasn't always like that.

He does not remember a childhood. From a young age, he was initiated into a local gang known for their extreme violence. They roamed the mountains, raiding villages, stealing, and killing. They drank the blood and ate the hearts of their victims, believing it gave them added powers. "We were cannibals," he said. "This was my life for many years." But deep in his heart, he knew there was something more.

A young evangelist with a big heart for the lost was also roaming the mountains, though with a completely different agenda. He had heard about Denunciano and believed he was to preach the gospel to this notorious gang leader. But how was he to get close to Denunciano? After much prayer, he took the extraordinary step of joining the gang. Even though he often witnessed to the members, no one threw him out. This went on for two years. Finally, the young evangelist told God, "I can't take this much longer. If Denunciano doesn't accept You by year three, release me of this assignment." And three days before year three, for the very last time, the evangelist asked Denunciano, "Will you go to church with me tonight?"

Much to his surprise, Denunciano said yes. The rest is history. Not only did Denunciano accept Jesus into his heart, but he also committed his life to telling others about his mercy and grace. "The ice in my heart and heaviness in my body disappeared," Denunciano said. "I felt like a newborn baby."

God immediately opened doors and worked miracles in his life. Though he was wanted for murder, all charges were dropped. He literally began running the mountainsides, telling everyone how much Jesus had done for him. At first people were afraid of him, but his radical, miraculous change soon brought many to Christ. Our team, too, was so grateful for Denunciano's strong arm and commitment to help the body of Christ.

Interestingly, in Spanish *denunciano* has a negative meaning—condemn, criticize, accuse—but also an appositive meaning—to declare, to tell, reveal—which illustrates Denunciano's past and present life before and after Christ. What a picture for each of our lives.

> And when Saul had come to Jerusalem, he tried to join the disciples; but they were all afraid of him and did not believe that he was a disciple. But Barnabas took him and brought him to the apostles. And he declared to them how he had seen the Lord on the road, and that He had spoken to him, and how he had preached boldly at Damascus in the name of Jesus. So he was with them at Jerusalem, coming in and going out. (Acts 9:26–28 NLT)

CHAPTER 18

Ministry Partners

*Now you are the body of Christ, and
each one of you is a part of it.*

1 Corinthians 12:27 NIV

We need each other! This simple truth was evidenced over and over. Some were called to pray, others gave finances, some donated goods, and still others joined hands to do the work. Together we fulfilled the Will Go mandate: Find a need and fill it; preach the gospel of Jesus Christ.

Missions school concluded shortly after the Mexico mission trip with a grand graduation. Pastor Billy Joe Daugherty exhorted us all to "run our race to the finish." However, our biggest concern was getting off the starting line!

A Bus Bully

Working as a missionary required multiple financial partners. New Covenant, our home church, had pledged their help, but we needed more support. Larry heard that Craig Vote had begun pastoring the United Evangelical Covenant Church in Harcourt, Iowa, and wanted to call him. But there was a problem.

Larry told me he used to bully Craig on the school bus and cause him all kinds of trouble. "I'm sure he remembers,"

Larry said. We decided to try calling anyway. It must have been quite a picture, both of us wedged into our overstuffed yellow chair, Larry nervously holding the rotary dial phone in one hand and me slowly dialing each number. After a couple of rings, Pastor Craig answered the phone. Larry explained what we had in our hearts to do.

"I'll bring it up to the church council tomorrow evening and let you know," Craig said and hung up.

Sunday night, eleven o'clock, and the phone was ringing. Pastor Craig told us he couldn't wait till morning to call. The church was on board with monthly support for our mission work. That news bolstered our faith; we now had two supporting churches and were ready to go.

And yes, Pastor Craig remembered those old bus days. But he said, "We recognize that God has made all things new." They not only supported financially, but he and his wife, Karen, also brought teams to China to help with our geriatric seminars and other outreaches. And our journey together continues. Hallelujah!

> Therefore, if anyone is in Christ, the new creation has come: The old has gone, the new is here. (2 Corinthians 5:17 NIV)

Incidentally, our last China trip with Pastor Craig and Karen necessitated a stopover in Hong Kong before flying home. To save money, we decided to share a room at the YMCA. However, the two beds turned out to be one double bed and a small single bed. Pastor Craig would not take no for an answer and slept on the cement floor. Shortly after returning home, he suffered a severe case of pneumonia. We felt so guilty, knowing that the dampness of Hong Kong and the cold cement floor contributed to this bout of illness. Craig exemplifies Proverbs 18:24:

But there is a friend who sticks closer than a brother.

Jesus Loves Me (and You)

During the transitional phase to full-time missions, I continued to work as a nurse, a job I loved. Many days were routine but not always. One morning's patient assignment would set up circumstances that only God could orchestrate. Mr. Beckman was suffering from end-stage cancer and had been admitted to our floor for supportive care. His beautiful young wife, Lavonne, and their two children were already in the room when I entered to begin morning assessments. Their deep love and respect for this man kept them camped out with food and pillows at his bedside day and night.

When I came into the room a few mornings later, two things were immediately evident. Mr. Beckman was very weak, and his family was exhausted. As his primary nurse, I decided to give his morning bath instead of passing it off to a nursing assistant and convinced Lavonne to take her children down to the cafeteria for a break. Reluctantly, they left, and I began caring for Mr. Beckman.

Only a few minutes had passed when I suddenly realized he was dying. I quickly opened our door to see if anyone was available to retrieve the family from the cafeteria, but no one was in sight. I closed the door and returned to his bedside. As I took his hand, a childhood song came to my heart, and I began to quietly sing "Jesus Loves You" (Anna Bartlett Warner, 1859). When the song ended, Mr. Beckman had gone to his eternal home. Having promised the family to stay at his side till they returned, I did just that. It was the least I could do. Overwhelming guilt flooded my heart and mind for insisting they go.

What seemed like an eternity (though probably not more than ten minutes), they were back. Immediately, they knew and stood speechless. Finally, Lavonne asked, "What did you do?"

"I sang 'Jesus Loves Me' to him."

She replied, her lips quivering, "That's just what I wanted to do."

We all burst into tears. God began a bonding in our hearts that has continued for nearly three decades. We did not know that Lavonne was a member of Pastor Craig's United Evangelical Covenant Church. When he shared our intentions to go into full-time missions, she immediately became a supporter and continues to this day. Only God.

> Who is like you, Lord God Almighty? You, Lord,
> are mighty, and your faithfulness surrounds you.
> (Psalm 89:8 NIV)

Stick a Leaf in Your Ear

I nearly fainted. Larry and I were sharing our mission work at New Life Family Church in Burlington (Pastor Richard and Diana Dutzer) when, suddenly, Larry said he had a word from the Lord. "There is someone here with ear problems. God said to roll up a green leaf, stick it in your ear, and you will be healed."

My first thought was *You've got to be kidding.* Did I mention that there was a designated section for the hearing impaired, with a sign language interpreter? Or that Pastor Dutzer had just announced they would begin supporting our work on a monthly basis? Somehow, we finished out the morning service and went back to our hotel room for the afternoon.

We were just beginning the evening service when a lady came running into the church shouting, "I'm healed, I'm healed." She went on to testify that she had been experiencing a severe ear infection for more than six months. Nothing had helped, so she took God's word and acted on it. In fact, she rolled up two green leaves, put one in each ear, and then lay down for a nap. When she woke up, she pulled the leaf out of her infected ear. It had turned completely yellow. From that moment on, her ear infection was completely healed.

God is incredible, and may I add, has a sense of humor too. *Really, God? Stick a leaf in your ear?*

Later Larry confided in me that he struggled to give that word too. He wasn't oblivious to the hearing-impaired section. But every time he tried to shove it out of his mind, it flew right back. Finally, he said, "OK, God, I trust You." Consequently, a suffering lady received her healing, and Pastor Dutzer's church began supporting us monthly, which continues to this day.

We were ready for the next step.

What Next? Oklahoma Again

Mission school was completed, and we were anxious to start serving God. Our first offer came from a Tulsa video ministry, and we took it. The director promised to teach us about video production, but after a year, it was clear our role was to carry equipment and babysit their children. Though the ministry of helps is vital, evangelism was in our hearts. God kept reminding Larry: "I called you to be a fisher of men." We cried out to God for the next step.

Sunday morning, we attended service as usual at Victory in Tulsa. "Go ye into the whole world," Pastor Billy Joe Daugherty declared and made a plea for help in Albania. We answered the call. Less than a month later, we landed in Tirane, the capital of Albania.

CHAPTER 19

Albania

Albania—This beautiful country, with a population just over three million in 1993, is nestled above Greece. The Dinaric Alps majestically adorn the northern border while the beautiful blue Adriatic Sea separates them from Italy. But the greatest beauty were the people themselves. They had suffered much yet were resilient and strong . . . perhaps in part by the years of prayers the European community had offered on their behalf. Many organizations had planned and prepared to help their little neighbor; as soon as the door opened, they were on the doorstep with food and multiple aids. We were privileged to work with some of them: Gesina Blaauw, founder of God Loves Albania, Besa Shapllo of Mission Possible, and many others. Our Victory Bible School students were sought after by many groups to help plant their work. It was a precious time with Christians from around the globe working arm in arm.

However, here we would experience the highest and lowest point in our ministry walk.

> So be truly glad. There is wonderful joy ahead, even though you must endure many trials for a little while. These trials will show that your faith is genuine. It is being tested as fire tests and purifies gold—though

your faith is far more precious than mere gold. So
when your faith remains strong through many trials,
it will bring you much praise and glory and honor
on the day when Jesus Christ is revealed to the
whole world. (1 Peter 1:6–7 NLT)

We entered the country just as they were emerging from
fifty years of isolation under communistic rule. Evidence of
anger and frustration visibly played out—school windows
smashed, orchards cut down, and broken glass was strewn
across the beaches. Ugly, nearly indestructible igloo-shaped
concrete bunkers, with pointed spears sticking out the top,
dotted the land—reminders of the brutal repression they
endured. But as the gospel was preached, hope arose in many
hearts, and healing began.

After a citywide crusade in Tirane, led by Pastor Billy
Joe Daughtery and his Victory Christian Center team (Tulsa,
Oklahoma), a Victory, Albania, church and Bible school were
established. We were some of the missionaries sent to carry on
the work. It was pure joy to work with these new Christians
whose hearts were like a fallow field. And amazingly, most
spoke multiple languages and easily grasped English.

However, living conditions were extremely difficult in
1993. Food choices were limited, telephones were found only in
a central exchange building, and few people owned a vehicle.
Taxis were old Mercedes, no longer allowed in Germany but
welcomed in Albania. Items we took for granted in North
America were nearly impossible to buy. Toilet paper, common
nails, or a paper cup took days to locate. We still thank God for
the Coca-Cola Company (yes, Coke was already there), who
willingly donated hundreds of paper cups for our outreaches.
Our days were filled with teaching and multiple ministry

assignments. We loved making home visits, which always included tiny cups of strong Albanian coffee. Life was good. It seemed nothing could go wrong . . .

Testing So Soon?

We were asked to expand the Victory ministry to Kombinat, six kilometers southwest of Tirana and had rented an upstairs apartment from a multigenerational Muslim family. They continued to live on the ground floor. The home was situated inside a gated cement wall about a ten-minute walk up a steep hill. Just down the hill was a tiny bakery. Each morning the aroma of freshly baked bread from the wood-fired oven wafted up to our room. The shop owner also sold butter from a huge block. He would cut off a hunk, weigh it, then wrap it in paper like a piece of meat. Breakfast was served.

It had been an exciting week with a grand Christmas party for our village kids and food and clothing outreaches with God Loves Albania. Everything had gone smoothly, and hundreds heard about God's son, Jesus.

And then *that* phone call came.

It was about nine o'clock at night on Christmas Eve when a runner from the center told us we had a phone call from the USA. The only phone for international calls was in a building about five minutes down the hill. We hurried down, happily thinking one of our kids was calling to wish us Merry Christmas.

But it was Janis Carmody, our pastor's wife. Her message was brief. "Jared's in the hospital here in Fort Dodge," she said. "He underwent emergency surgery for a leaky appendix last night." She didn't have many details, gave us the hospital's phone number, and hung up. We were stunned; slowly we trudged the dark path back up the hill and quietly entered our compound. Our strong, twenty-year-old son in the hospital? He was supposed to be in Chicago at Christian Life College. We prayed half the night. Larry told me if I wanted to go back, I should. However, international flights from Tirana were not daily. We had no choice but to wait.

Jared's Unforgettable Words

Morning finally came. After a few attempts, our international call went through, and the nurse linked us to Jared's room. He sounded weak but was emphatic that we should remain in Albania. His exact words: "If God can raise His Son from the dead, surely He can raise your son from his sickbed." His faith and confidence gave us peace. We stayed in Albania. And Jared was surrounded with family and friends.

The Home Team

The NCCC family in Fort Dodge jumped in with prayers, visits, and helps of all kinds. Flowers and balloons overflowed Jared's room out to the hallway. We did not have hospital insurance, but God came to the rescue again. Sue Moeller (though no longer married to my brother Art) took up Jared's cause. His surgery, ICU, and ten-day stay had pushed the bill into tens of thousands of dollars. Sue researched and petitioned a local charity, and by God's grace, they paid the entire bill. We were overwhelmed with the goodness of God again.

> I will praise You with my whole heart; before the gods I will sing praises to You. (Psalm 138:1)

Back to Albania and the Victory Team

It was a privilege to be part of such a dedicated team. Teaching in the Victory Bible School was a joy. The students loved the

Word of God. One drawback, however, was their lack of trust for anyone outside their immediate family. Fifty years of communist rule had instilled much fear. When Lumteri, a little mountain girl, wanted to come to Bible school, it was a big problem.

Lumteri's Story

Lumteri loved God and had somehow heard about our Victory Bible School in Tirana. She wanted to attend but had no place to stay. We tried to pay several different families to keep her, but the answer was always no. Everyone was afraid of her brothers, whom they felt would steal from them. Finally, we decided to keep her. However, that proved to be difficult too. We were still living above our Muslim family in Kombinat, and when they heard we were taking her in, they threatened to throw us out. We asked them to give us a one-week trial. Within that short time, Lumteri won the landlords' trust.

The first English words she learned were "I'm not hungry." She felt so embarrassed because she was staying for free that she tried to fast the whole week. Finally, we had Keti Abazi, our translator, explain to her that everything we had was provided by God, and she was entitled to it too. Finally, she ate.

Lumteri graduated from Bible school and loves God today. Facebook allows us to stay connected.

Thoughts on Marriage from Lumteri's Brother

Lumteri's brother attended Bible school for a semester and took the class on Christian marriage. When test time came, one of the questions was "Name two main qualities you would look for in a mate." Of course, we were looking for answers such as one who loves God, follows His ways, and raises a family to know God. So you could imagine our surprise to read his answers: strong back, sound teeth. Certainly, the hardships of mountain life change one's priorities. We hope he married a strong wife who loved God too.

Mirgen's Story

Mirgen Dhima, one of our Bible school students, also attended another university majoring in design. He asked if we could talk with his dad, because he had forbidden him to continue in the Bible school. His dad felt he couldn't keep up with studies at two places. So we made the journey to his village. When we entered their home, it was clear that Mirgen was quite nervous. His father was sitting on the other side of the room with a serious look on his face. After talking for some time, his father still did not give consent for Bible school. Finally, Larry opened the Bible and read aloud from Exodus 20, "Honor your father and mother." Mirgen looked incredulous. Larry explained that he knew his father cared deeply for Mirgen and just wanted the best for his son.

But he also said that God is a father, too, and wants the best for His children. "Let's give Mirgen a chance," Larry said to the father. "If his university grades drop while he is in the Bible school, I will personally forbid him to continue."

That afternoon, with those stipulations in place, Mirgen's father agreed. Mirgen excelled greatly in both schools. Today, he honors God through his successful graphic design business, inWeb.AL, in Tirana.

A Trip to Germany

Luan Xhemalaj, Yili Velija, and Ilir Pinari, our pastor-leaders, had been so faithful and hardworking, showing up for every outreach, church service, and team meeting, that Larry felt it would be wonderful to treat them to a pastors conference in Germany. Pastor James Kennedy from Florida was the keynote speaker, and many pastors from all over Europe were attending. His first preaching was a powerful salvation message. Ilir whispered to Larry, "Why is he preaching about salvation? We are all pastors." When Pastor Kennedy asked for those who wanted to be saved to come forward, the altar was full. God knew what was needed.

We so appreciated Luan, Yili, and Ilir, who helped expand the ministry through their sheer love for God and willingness to serve.

> If you declare with your mouth, "Jesus is Lord," and believe in your heart that God raised him from the dead, you will be saved. (Romans 10:9 NIV)

Evangelism was our primary focus. God gave Larry the idea to set up home Sunday schools, donating five dollars weekly to city families willing to host a children's meeting in their neighborhood. Because many still struggled with poverty, it was a win-win cooperation. Pastor Iler completely caught the vision and dedicated a whole room in his home for the kids. Pastor Luan and other Victory Bible School students also flew Mission Aviation Fellowship (MAF) helicopters to remote regions of the Albanian Alps, making sure those children could know Jesus too.

A deep-rooted love for the Albanian people continued to grow in our hearts. We were willing to serve them all the days of our lives, and that door seemed to be opening.

Pastor Greg Warner, head over Victory Albania, asked Larry to marry him to the love of his life, fellow missionary Libbet. They returned to the States, leaving us in charge. The following year, Pastor Billy Joe Daugherty brought a big team for a third Albanian crusade inside the iconic Enver Hoxha marble pyramid. By this time, minds had shifted. Families were more interested in programs for their children. Those events were packed beyond capacity. And God gave Pastor Billy Joe a rare gift. He was able to witness the fruit of his first Albanian crusade. Victory Bible School graduates who only a few years earlier had rushed forward to receive salvation now formed a dedicated ground team, helping Billy Joe bring new souls into the kingdom. The fruit had not only remained but was active and well!

> I am the vine; you are the branches. If you remain in me and I in you, you will bear much fruit; apart from me you can do nothing. (John 15:5 NIV)

Our Kombinat Family

As mentioned earlier, we lived in the upstairs rooms of a Muslim family. Two brothers with their wives, children, and elderly mother lived below. They were a friendly family that clearly loved each other. Of course, they had keys to the upstairs, which led to some surprises.

The spit shine

Since we were gone all day, our host family agreed to clean our house. They kept everything gleaming. One day, we arrived home early and witnessed the cleaning process. When little Ariana caught our eye, she smiled proudly and with a bit of gusto spat several times on the table and vigorously wiped it with her cloth. What could we say? We smiled back . . . and remembered to wash the table with soap and water.

Splish splash

The brothers had installed a nice big shower upstairs, which we assumed was for our private use. One afternoon, we ran back home to pick up some things and found half the family in the shower. I'm not sure who was most surprised. We learned it was the home's sole shower and sharing was the only option. We were part of the family.

A sewing beginning

What was all the excitement about an old treadle sewing machine? Both husbands enthusiastically waved us into the room where they stood watching their wives take turns operating the new sewing machine. They insisted I take a turn too, clapping and whistling each time the machine whirled into action. The excitement was more than a kid's experience on Christmas Day. And why not? It marked a new beginning. They had moved into the machine age: no longer did they have to make and mend all their clothing by hand. The year was 1994.

Peroxide and erythromycin

Little Arben was happily riding on the back of his father's bicycle as they flew down the hill to Kombinat. How it happened no one really knows, but his foot got tangled in the spokes of the bike. The family rushed him to the doctor. To everyone's relief, there were no broken bones, but the foot was badly mangled with several open wounds. A few days later, Arben's mother asked me to look at the foot. She had noticed a red streak up his leg, and he was running a temperature. The wound smelled horrible and oozed yellow matter. It needed immediate attention, and so donning my "nurse's cap," we began. His mother and auntie tried to hold him still as I painstakingly debrided and cleaned his wounds, but nothing could stop his pitiful screams. Thankfully, I had packed peroxide, triple antibiotic ointment, and erythromycin capsules from the States—in fact, enough antibiotic doses for ten days (There were no antibiotics in Albania at that time.) We continuously thank God for His divine setups. We lived in the right place at the right time to help little Arben. What a wonderful God we serve.

A few years later, we visited Albania and Arben's family. The first thing Arben did was throw off his shoes and socks and show us his foot. Some scars, yes, but perfectly fine. And better yet, Arben and his sister were still attending the Victory church.

> Your righteousness, God, reaches to the heavens,
> you who have done great things.
> Who is like you, God?
> (Psalm 71:19 NIV)

More Friends

Several friends traveled from the USA to assist us with the work. Vy Bates came by herself on her first mission trip. She was a sweet encouragement. Larry and Janet Rhoton and Brad and Kim Bendickson followed, teaching in the Bible school, ministering in so many ways. And Carl Kennedy, of Tulsa, Oklahoma, a graduate of Oral Roberts University, joined us numerous times. He connected with the students and continued contact for many years. His extraordinary gift of teaching, coupled with his personal heartache and testimony, resonated deeply with the people.

We are forever grateful for these precious teams. However, change was coming—sooner than we thought.

> Every branch in Me that does not bear fruit He takes away; and every branch that bears fruit He prunes, that it may bear more fruit. (John 15:2)

It was another beautiful morning in Albania with the usual rooster's crow, dogs' barking, and smell of buke (bread) fresh from the wood-fired oven down the lane. John 15:2 was the focus verse for our morning devotions. God seemed to be speaking about change. Little did we know that within a few months, we would be chopped, pruned from Albania. The vine has no say when the vinedresser decides to cut away a branch. And so it was with us.

Three months later, we received notice to meet with a Victory representative at one of Tirana's finest restaurants. The decor was beautiful with white linen-like cloths on each small table. As Larry and I were being seated, we watched our host carefully take off his coat and, with a flourish, hang it on the back of his chair. He then stretched and gingerly sat on the edge of his seat. This bizarre action reminded me of a boxer throwing off his cape before stepping into the ring. We were told to order anything we liked.

And then just before the food arrived, we were fired. No reason was given, yet we felt we had been accused of something. We said nothing. Our firing brother looked relieved and seemed to relax a bit. He had evidently imagined quite a different response.

Larry's heart was crushed. Though that deep-rooted love could never be extinguished, it felt as if his arm had been ripped out of the socket; he loved the students and church like his own children. We drank Albanian coffee with family after family, week after week, and throughout each day, these precious people were in our hearts. But we had no choice, and on Christmas Day 1995, we flew back to the USA. We had served there two years and nine months.

God Knows All Things

We originally went to missions school to prepare to serve in Asia, specifically China. And we were also sure that God had called us for a season in Albania. However, one thing we had not learned yet: God knows when you are finished, even if you don't. In hindsight, we had to step into China at just that time for the specific plans He had for us. He is a set-up God. And at times, that might mean an upset.

> Many are the plans in a person's heart, but it is the Lord's purpose that prevails. (Proverbs 19:21 NIV)

Again, the Precious Body of Christ

We were upset and searching for answers. We decided to join the Holy Life Tabernacle Pastors Conference, hosted by Pastors Dave and Jeanne Kaufman in South Dakota. We were sitting far in the back when the speaker, Dwight Fearing from Sisseton, suddenly stopped and called us up front. He said, "God sees, and He will vindicate you." He spoke those same words several times and then went on with his preaching. We were greatly encouraged. No one there knew our situation, but from that time on, a peace that only God can bring settled in our hearts. We knew He knew. Pastor Dwight's church took the extra step to add us to their missions support. It continues to this day.

Not long after we received that vindicating word from God, Victory's head pastor, Billy Joe Daugherty (who pastored over 12,000 members and guarded his time carefully) called us for a personal meeting. We had been asked to join a Victory missions work in the Czech Republic, but after dutifully checking it out, we declined. Billy Joe, not one to beat around the bush, looked directly at us and asked, "Why didn't you go to the Czech Republic?"

Larry answered simply, "God called us to China, not the Czech Republic."

Pastor Billy Joe stood up and said, "That's good enough for me," and prayed a blessing over us. Victory Christian Center continued their monthly support for another twenty years, even after precious Pastor Billy Joe died.

Though we never learned what had prompted our dismissal from Albania, we could echo the words Joseph had spoken to his brothers in Genesis 50:20 (NIV):

> You intended to harm me, but God intended it for good to accomplish what is now being done, the saving of many lives.

We, too, could say, *This was God's doing*. So be it.

CHAPTER 20

The People's Republic of China

China—China is the world's most populous country with nearly 1.5 billion people. Perhaps no country on earth has recreated itself in such a short time. Bicycles, yellow taxicabs, and slow railway systems were the norm of 1990s, and most housing consisted of gray cement six-story buildings without elevators. Today, bullet trains reaching speeds of 217 mph connect more than 550 cities through thirty-three of the country's thirty-four provinces, and high-rise buildings of beautiful and unique architecture are found in every major city. China is the undisputed manufacturing capital of the world. But underneath all the glamour and worldly progress, a spiritual hunger remains. Underground churches continue to grow. Officially, 44 million Christians live in China. However, Freedom House, a US human rights group, estimates the number closer to 100 million. We can attest that the gospel is alive and well and that our brothers and sisters are resilient, hardworking, and apply godly wisdom in their approach to problems. This is evident in their resolve to protect and expand the gospel. One precious brother told us, "We are not afraid of suffering— we expect to suffer." Be inspired by their stories—God's mighty hand at work. They are forever in our hearts.

Our hope was to be on Chinese soil by the spring of 1996, so we focused on adding prayer and financial partners. When we shared our heart at Christian Life Church in the Chicago area, Joel Holms, who was translating Bible school materials into Mandarin for underground churches, approached us and asked, "Do you know anyone in China?" We did not. He then asked, "What will you do when you get there?" Again, we did not know. We just knew that God said to go, so we agreed that we would go.

"I know someone who might help you," Joel said, "but he is busy helping many foreigners, so there is no guarantee. I'll send him a fax, but there's not time to get an answer back. If he can help, he will be at the airport to meet you. His English name is David."

In faith we had purchased two tickets to Beijing. Our "no plan" was the agenda. Though we had researched various cities, history, and cultural aspects, we knew the most important thing was to hear God's voice and move accordingly. On a cool, cloudy day in early April 1996, we drove to the Minneapolis International Airport and boarded a Northwest Airlines (now merged with Delta) flight to Beijing. Over the next twenty-one hours, we moved from excitement to dread, from *Thank you, Lord* to *Where are you taking us, Lord?* And round and round again. As we touched the tarmac in Beijing, moved toward customs, and heard the chop-chop of the entry stamp pressed into our passports, a supernatural peace engulfed us. Through His strength, we could face whatever lay ahead.

And there he was! David, a slightly balding, middle-aged Chinese man, stood smiling in the welcoming line holding a simple handwritten sign that read, "Mr. and Mrs. Johnson." With relief and gratitude to God, we thanked him for picking us up. Since it was late afternoon, we stopped for dinner. As

The Great Wall of China—the journey begins.

we browsed the menu, David asked in perfect English, "Do you like fungus?" We looked at each other and smiled; of course, he meant mushrooms.

David was a wonderful help during our first years in China. He testified to us that as he laid his hands on Joel's fax, God had spoken to his heart and said, *You must help them get planted in China.*

With that mandate, he arranged to be with us every day for one month. It was both a joy and comfort to hear him state each morning, "This is the plan for today." We traveled by train to Shenzhen and Shanghai and several smaller cities. Bicycles, yellow taxicabs, and slow railway systems were the norm of the nineties.

Then one day, David began talking to us about the ancient city of Kaifeng. "This place is really dear to my heart," he said. "I hope you will pray about locating there."

Kites and Jews

Kaifeng is China's kite-making capital. But that is not all. Kaifeng, as we were to learn, is also home to the Chinese Jew. They had originally migrated along the Silk Road during the Tang dynasty. The emperor gave Babylonian and Persian Jews his blessing and allowed them to settle in Kaifeng for business. A Jewish community was established; however, favor is not always guaranteed, and during the Cultural Revolution (1966–1976), the government tried to rid China of any Jewish history. Certainly, God's protective hand was on His people. Every Jew was required to give up their original documents and government cards, which were replaced with new identity cards. However, some of the older ladies sat on their documents and told the police they were lost or already collected. By God's grace, we can still see a remnant of Jewish ancestry in China today.

David, who had a heart for Jewish people, hoped we would agree to settle in Kaifeng and start a work there, but we could not get peace to do so. We needed to heed our own mandate: follow the peace in your heart, even above the ideas and rationale in your mind. Every time we crossed back into Beijing, we felt at home, and so it was there near the North Third Ring Road that we settled into work.

He replied, "Blessed rather are those who hear the word of God and obey it." (Luke 11:28 NIV)

Student Visas

How do you stay in a foreign country, especially a country where you cannot declare you are a missionary? It was illegal for us to openly preach to anyone. Again, David came to the rescue. Because of his special *guanxi* (relationships), we were able to receive student visas to study Chinese. We were in our fifties and may have been some of the oldest students ever to study in a Chinese college. Our dorm room was the size of a cheap hotel room with two twin beds, a small table, two chairs, and a desk. We added a Crock-Pot. This space was our home for the next eighteen months.

Our main heart and hope was that our college teachers would hear and accept the gospel. During this time, our first team came from NCCC in Iowa. Andy and Janice Birkland, Doug and Diana Bacon, Vy Bates, and Lee Rosenquist helped us host a beautiful dinner party for our college teachers and students. Seeds were planted.

David's Testimony

David's testimony is a wonderful example of God's providence and provision. When the Cultural Revolution began, David

We loved our teachers—Larry and Professor Xi.

was a university professor. Every person, regardless of status or educational level, was issued their own copy of Chairman Mao's *Little Red Book* and was required to memorize it.

The Little Red Book, intended to be kept in your pocket, was about five inches in size and bound in bright red vinyl. The contents, considered sacred, were attributed to Mao Zedong, founder of the People's Republic of China and then chairman of the Communist Party. It was to become the dominant ideology preserving communism by purging capitalist and traditional elements. The Red Army, composed of university-age youth, had been empowered by Chairman Mao to enforce the learning of his book and to disrupt or destroy all artifacts, buildings, books, and even people considered traditional. During this period more than 85,000 families were forced out of their homes in Beijing alone, and targeted massacres erased twenty-two long-standing families from the land.

During that chaotic interval, David found himself in another mandatory memorization session of *The Little Red Book*. It was a morning like hundreds before it. Compulsory reviewing and reciting of Chairman Mao's book took precedence. David, with his photographic memory, had already memorized the 427 quotes months earlier and struggled with sheer boredom. That fateful day, the class monitor discovered David with his "precious" *Red Book* upside down. He asked him, "Why do you have Chairman Mao's book upside down?"

David (who admittedly confessed he had wanted to show off his capabilities) boldly responded, "I know this book inside out, upside down, and right-side up."

The monitor sternly admonished him, "David, you know Chairman Mao too much."

At lunchtime, he noticed that no one would sit by him or even come near the table. Later that afternoon, he was arrested and taken to the cattle shed. The cattle shed was designated for those who no longer had "human status" but were considered animals. Many times, the authorities marched David's wife and two young sons by the shed to see "the animal," forcing them to pelt him with curses and rocks. Punishment also included standing for hours in the airplane position, where the body was bent over at the waist and arms held straight behind the back, with one hand grasping the other at the wrist. He suffered permanent back injury from this torture. However, other prisoners who could not memorize well, due to low education or inability to read, were forced to stay in this position many more hours than himself; hearing their cries for mercy was another terrible suffering. Food was near starvation rations; many, many prisoners died alone in the cattle shed.

During this dark time, one good thing happened. "The university gardener, another prisoner in the cattle shed, persistently shared Jesus with me," David recounted with a smile. "Don't tell me about Jesus; I don't need any more trouble" was his fearful response, but the seeds were planted.

Eventually, David was released and went back home, though it took years to repair the relationship with his sons. The words of propaganda had had a profound effect on them.

We do not know for sure when David accepted Jesus as his personal Savior, but his life's mission was to help Christians, especially those who wanted to live in China and share the gospel. He called himself the Burden Bearer. This unique servant was not through opening doors for us. While we were studying Chinese, he asked if we would consider teaching a special program to prepare high school students to study in the USA. We immediately agreed and began the three-month course. We were given the freedom to develop the curriculum

A thank-you gift for David, the Burden Bearer.

to include culture, holidays, and religious beliefs. Thankfully, most of the students were already fluent in English. It was a wonderful window of opportunity for the gospel.

Special Students
Since we were not sure the program would continue for the full three months, Larry decided to share the gospel during our first week of teaching. He carefully outlined the steps of salvation on the blackboard and told them that God loved them so much that He would send us teachers from the other side of the world to tell them this good news. Larry asked, "Do you believe this? Do you accept Jesus as your Savior?" All thirty-four students raised their hands to accept Jesus.

> Then Peter began to speak: "I now realize how true it is that God does not show favoritism but accepts from every nation the one who fears him and does what is right. You know the message God sent to the people of Israel, announcing the good news of peace through Jesus Christ, who is Lord of all." (Acts 10:34–36 NIV)

That very night, one of the top students, Bai Hao, came to our hotel room with his father and said, "Larry, I want you to tell my dad what you told us in class today about Jesus." We were quite alarmed by this surprise visit. We didn't know who they were or what authority they may have. However, Larry carefully outlined the salvation plan to Bai Hao's dad, who simply said, "Thank you, this is good." He said he would allow Bai Hao to continue studying with us. Later his son received a visa to study at a high school in the USA. Amazingly, he was placed in a school only a few miles from Larry's sister in Missouri. God arranged for us to attend his high school graduation.

One of our students, Bai Hao.

It is thrilling to see the enthusiasm of a new Christian. Bai Hao introduced us to his cousin, Bai Yong Hao, and girlfriend, and they also accepted Jesus and studied the Bible with us for a year. Later they married and reside in China to this day.

A Stumble in the Road

During the second month of our teaching, Bai Hao invited us to his far north hometown of Harbin to see the famous winter ice sculptures. The second day, he arranged a trip to the Japanese palace. The taxi dropped us off at the bottom of a steep walkway and took off. It was extremely cold and icy, but we made it to the top, only to find the palace was closed. On the way back down, I fell and broke my leg.

At the time, I did not know that both bones above the ankle were fractured. It took nearly an hour to hobble to the main road and flag down a taxi. Bai Hao assured us that we would go to the best hospital in Harbin. However, on arrival, we found the hospital did not own a wheelchair. Larry and the students helped me get up on a dirty, paint-chipped utility cart, and I was rolled into the emergency room. We were together in one room with multiple other patients, each in their own distressful state. Larry was ushered to the financial department and paid a $200 USD fee, allowing me to see the doctor. When the doctor ordered x-rays, he had to go again and pay more money before that could proceed. The old x-ray machine groaned and took many seconds to record. Bai Hao and the other students were lined up around me; no one mentioned they should leave the room. Pain medications were not available, even with cash. Every movement was excruciating.

The doctor told us my leg needed to be pinned and plated and he would arrange the surgery after the weekend. We considered the terrible, unsanitary conditions and made the decision to return to Beijing. The doctor was openly angry with our decision but said he would apply a cast—of course, after Larry paid more money. All this time Bai Hao had been translating for us. When I learned how much money Larry had paid, I said in English, "I could have had two casts for that price in the US."

The doctor immediately retorted in perfect English, "I'll give you another cast." He proceeded to cut off the first cast and reapply a second. When he finished, he said, "Now you have two casts for the price of one."

Larry had warned me in English to be careful what I said, but I didn't listen.

He who guards his mouth preserves his life, but
he who opens wide his lips shall have destruction.
(Proverbs 13:3)

It was a very painful lesson.

Bai Hao and his father arranged for us to fly back to Beijing that evening. We had nowhere else to go but our dorm room, which was on the sixth floor. With no elevator, the journey up was slow and painful. The hospital also did not have any crutches, so I hopped up every step. The next day, we were advised to go to the Japanese hospital in Beijing, where the doctor confirmed that surgery was needed for this type of break but would not consider it. He stated, "There are no antibiotics available in China that can fight bone infection." He recommended we fly back to the States as soon as possible.

However, we still had six weeks left to instruct our students. God had given us such a love for them, and we wanted to help ground them in the Bible, so we decided to stay. The manager of the program was so grateful that we would continue that he moved the class to the hotel meeting room. He also arranged for high school boys from a nearby school to carry me up and down the six flights of stairs. A team of six were assigned this duty—two students per two flights. Up and down (me seated on a straight wooden chair) we went for six weeks. And more help was about to materialize.

Zhang KaiQing

At that time, we barely knew the university cook, Zhang KaiQing. "I'll find crutches for you," he said. And for three days, he pedaled the school's utility bicycle from one end of Beijing to the other searching for a pair of matching crutches, at that time a rare luxury item. His persistence paid off, and with a big smile, he delivered them to our dorm room. Once again, God provided through an unexpected source.

Tracy Cui

She was an amazing student, fluent in English and beautiful inside and out. Tracy's home was in Tianjin, so she and her mom, Hong Lin, rented a bed space in a large dormitory near our Beijing school. Our visit to that dorm opened our eyes to the sacrifice people are willing to make to better themselves. Pallid light from a small broken window helped camouflage the stark black iron bunkbeds. Squatty potty toilets, void of any enclosures, lined one side of the bathroom and faced a multi-functional trough shared by forty or fifty ladies for bathing and washing clothes. Hong Lin endured these conditions, protecting her young daughter while she attended our preparatory classes.

Some of our most cherished times were hosting Tracy and her mom in our dorm home for supper. We filled the Crock-Pot with ham, carrots, potatoes, onion, and cabbage;

borrowed chairs from other rooms; and set out four bowls with disposable wooden chopsticks on our tiny round table. Drinking water, still piping hot, was poured into teacups from the hotel thermos delivered each morning to our room. Conversation flowed easily with Tracy translating for her mom. Our friendship continued to blossom.

Spring Festival

Chinese Spring Festival, commonly known in the US as Chinese New Year, is a dazzling celebration. Millions of people travel from coast to coast to visit relatives and friends, filling trains and packing roadways. Major banks are closed for at least one week. Tiananmen Square bursts with a diverse group of people from many provinces taking pictures, flying colorful kites, and eating. Parks are alive with music, dragon dances, food, and decorations, especially the red lantern. During this holiday, we learned how to make Chinese dumplings (*jiao za*), play mah-jongg (developed during the Qing dynasty), and eat specialty foods from a stick.

Because so many Chinese worked far from their hometowns or at very demanding jobs, Spring Festival was the only holiday with enough time to reconnect with family and friends. The following year, during this special time, we had the privilege of meeting Tracy's father.

Tracy's Father

Tracy had accepted the Lord during Larry's presentation that first week of our USA preparatory school and attended our fellowship gatherings. The following Spring Festival, she invited us to her hometown of Tianjin, another huge Chinese city eighty-five miles southeast of Beijing. It was a wonderful time of specialty foods (her mom, Hong Lin, is a great cook) and beautiful walks. But the most memorable moment came when Tracy shared the impact of her father's words before she left for our school in Beijing: "If you ever find an American who wants to tell you about Jesus, listen." His words opened her heart to the gospel.

> He also taught me and said to me: "Let your heart retain my words; keep my commands, and live" (Proverbs 4:4).

As soon as the last six weeks of our teaching finished, we flew back to the USA to have my leg checked out. US doctors said it was healing fine and confirmed the Chinese doctor had done an excellent job. They also agreed the best option was to plate and pin it, but the rebreaking, surgical procedure, and rehab would delay our return to China for at least six months. The alternative? Live with an imperfect leg half an inch shorter than the other. We chose the latter and made plans to return to China. But before we left, God arranged another special meeting.

The White House, Washington, DC

Mike and Cindy Mulroney, our friends from NCCC in Fort Dodge, surprised us with an invitation to speak at the White House. They arranged all the details, including security passes, through their DC connections.

Our speaking date, August 19, 1996, happened to coincide with President Bill Clinton's fiftieth birthday. The route to our meeting took us by one of his mostly eaten birthday cakes. I couldn't resist and picked up a tiny morsel. We continued down the marble corridor to a beautiful, spacious room where many had gathered for weekly prayer. We shared our plans for the work in China, answered questions, and then the prayers began. They prayed for us, for China, for the USA, and more. It was humbling to be included and amazing to know godly men and women committed time each week to ask God's intervention in the affairs of the land.

And then back to Beijing.

BTV University Life
"It's not cold, Larry, is it?" asked Wang Laoshir (teacher Wang). She was dressed only in a light-weight sweater and pants. Our teeth were chattering, even though we were still wearing our winter coats. The government did not heat the university rooms, and since we had so few in our class, body heat was insufficient. We do not know how the teachers endured the cold. None of them ever wore a coat to class. Despite this hardship, they were great teachers and seemed to enjoy their jobs. It was through them that we learned some cultural lessons and jokes:

Culture lesson: Ten little birdies sitting in a row. First head up has to go.

All Chinese children quickly learn that conformity, not individuality, is key to survival. Standing up or standing out may not end well or as the person envisioned.

Joke: There was a farmer who needed a pair of shoes. His wife measured his foot with a piece of string and told him not to lose the string. "This is your foot measurement," she said. However, on the way to the shoe seller, he somehow lost the string. He timidly returned home without a pair of shoes. His wife berated him saying, "You fool, you may not have had the string, but you had your foot."

There were many husband-wife jokes with the wife depicted as the right or bright one. Culture again?

We did learn to speak some Chinese; it is a beautiful language with a fascinating history. Many of the characters clearly depicted an exceedingly early awareness of God and His Word. *The Gospel Hidden in Chinese Characters* by Timothy D. Boyle and *The Discovery of Genesis* by C. H. Kang are two books (Kindle edition) that give more insight.

We remember each of our teachers by name: Teachers Xi, Gao, Wang, and Xiao. Seeds were planted; we continue to pray they have taken root.

It was another routine day in Beijing. We had finished our morning classes and returned to the dorm to study. Suddenly, Larry's chair, with him seated on it, flew across the room and then right back. "What just happened?" Before we could answer our own question, a man came running down the hall, shouting that he had been thrown out of his bed. It was our first earthquake. The epicenter was about three hours from Beijing, where many homes were severely damaged. We purchased blankets and rice and traveled to one of the villages to distribute the helps and present the gospel. People were so open as Larry talked about life after death through Jesus. They readily accepted our Chinese language tracts explaining salvation. More seeds were planted.

BTV University Friends
Adrian Burri

We continue to stand in awe of God and His divine arrangements. We so appreciated Adrian and his wife, Joan, from the start. Adrian, a Swiss guy, was extremely gifted in language, mastering Chinese in less than two years—writing included. But he had other plans too. One night he came to our dorm room and asked if we would be his pastors. That simple act set up a chain of events.

THE PEOPLE'S REPUBLIC OF CHINA

Together, we began a Bible fellowship, and soon others joined. Michael and his friend Tom and Liu Wen and Mae were some of the first regulars. Larry met Michael and Tom while teaching English at the A&W fast-food chain, and Joan led Mae to the Lord while teaching English at an institute. Mae's boyfriend was Liu Wen.

Liu Wen and Mae

A group of college friends had planned a trip to the lake, but at the last minute, Liu Wen's current girlfriend could not go. Someone invited Mae. She had never met Liu Wen before, but they hit it off immediately. They swam together and talked for hours. "It just seemed right." she said. A short time later, they moved in together. Liu Wen had a tender heart and immediately started coming to fellowship. He, too, accepted the Lord; however, their living arrangements did not change.

One Sunday, Adrian was giving the Word. He shared Scriptures relating God's desire that we live holy lives and on the covenant of marriage. He stressed that God set up these structures to bless us and for us to be a blessing. Lui Wen was convicted and asked Mae to marry him. We'll never forget that day. They had invited many unsaved friends and asked Adrian and Larry to share the gospel. Their theme song was "Give Thanks with a Grateful Heart," written by Henry Smith (made famous by Don Moen). It would take a few more chapters to share all the ways Lui Wen and Mae have helped us and continue to bless the body of Christ.

Joan Burri

God was already paving a road we did not know we would walk. Adrian's wife, Joan, was from Hong Kong and would introduce us to Kam Leung and Lisa Wan, who had immigrated to Canada. However, at this time, we believed we would live all our days in China. In fact, we told our kids if they got a package of powder in the mail not to worry. It was just Mom or Dad coming home (cremated). More on Kam and Lisa later (years later).

Ralph Flory

Ralph, whom we met at BTV University, was from the Midwest with an interest in agriculture. He set up an agricultural company using the patents of antique farm equipment to make implements for the remote and mountainous areas of China. He was a great blessing to many country farmers. We introduced him to Heidi, and she became his poster girl for many years. Today, Ralph continues to live in Beijing, having married a sweet Chinese lady named Sarah. We remain connected in heart though far apart.

Mali Hua

In the early nineties, it was common for vendors to park on the street with their wooden carts filled with fresh produce. Mali Hua was the cute little sister of one such vendor. Every day, like clockwork, they were outside our building with their vegetables. We really enjoyed Mali and invited her to our newly formed Bible fellowship. She became a dear sister. She loved teaching Bible stories with the flannel board and later joined our Will Go representative office team to help with our geriatric work. Today, she manages her own business, while still loving and serving God.

A Chance Encounter

It was early spring. As Larry and I were walking near our school a man in his sixties rode up on a three-wheel delivery bicycle. He spoke perfect English and asked if we would like to come to his house, and he would tutor us in Chinese. We were a bit concerned because we didn't know who he was and, at that time, very few Chinese had such perfect English.

Molly loved to share the stories of Jesus.

However, Yang ZaiDoe insisted we come for tea and gave us his address. Very soon, we would discover that this was no chance encounter but another divine connection. His father had been a university professor, and because of that, he now lived in a spacious government apartment with an exceptionally large private library. However, life had not always been so comfortable for our new friend.

During the Cultural Revolution, Yang ZaiDoe was considered an intellectual and therefore an enemy of the state. He endured many "public criticisms," wearing a dunce cap and a sign draped around him that read "enemy of the state." These criticisms were held in large auditoriums in front of hundreds of people. The "dunce" was forced to recite his crimes over and over while enduring jeers and beatings. He also suffered daily interrogations and shock treatments. Many people did not survive. "They thought they could break me, but in fact, they never did," he related. "My faith in Jesus took me through."

On another visit, he told us he assumed he would be exempted from the Red Guard and the reeducation camps because his mother was Zhou Enlai's girlfriend. During that time, Zhou Enlai was the second highest official in the land, serving as premier of the People's Republic of China under Chairman Mao. "It shocked me greatly to learn my own mother, whom I loved deeply, had turned me in," he emotionally recounted. "And it did not end well for her. After Zhou Enlai broke off their relationship, Mother quickly spiraled into a deep depression and took her own life." Yang ZaiDoe told us this news hurt him more deeply than the taunts and beatings of the reeducation camps. He wrote a book depicting his journey of forgiveness toward his mother and the Red Guard and reflecting on his continued hope in God. Yang's

THE PEOPLE'S REPUBLIC OF CHINA

story reminds us that forgiveness is a powerful tool, a love gift from God.

> In Him we have redemption through His blood, the forgiveness of sins, according to the riches of His grace. (Ephesians 1:7)

> For I know that my Redeemer lives,
> And He shall stand at last on the earth;
> And after my skin is destroyed, this I know,
> That in my flesh I shall see God.
> (Job 19:25–26)

Heidi, God's Divine Connection

It was a great benefit to study Chinese with Yang ZaiDoe, but it certainly was not the only one. He was also tutoring Ding HaiWen (better known as Heidi), a young Chinese girl from Jiangsu province. Yang told her to go to our dorm room and offer to teach us Chinese in exchange for English. She did. We will never forget that day. When we opened our door, Heidi said in very broken English, "I . . . come . . . teach . . . you . . . Chinese."

Though her English was far too low for her to be an effective tutor, Larry felt the Holy Spirit's prompting to hire her. The great news is that after one month of studying the Gospel of John together, Heidi accepted the Lord as her personal Savior. Little did we know that meeting Heidi was part of God's divine plan for establishing Will Go in China.

At nineteen, Heidi traveled alone from her countryside home to Beijing, her dream since childhood. Because of limited finances, she rented a bunk bed from an old granny living in the hutong—narrow streets formed by low, tile-roofed houses with a center courtyard—behind our school.

In exchange for some of the rent, she would help Granny with washing and cooking.

Nighttime was a nightmare because the rats came out of hiding. Heidi told us Granny slept in the bottom bunk so she could tap her cane on the stone floor to keep the rats at bay. Through this hardship, God was building tenacity and character in Heidi.

One morning, Heidi's neighbor gave her a raw fish. Since she didn't have time to clean and cook it, she regifted it to another neighbor in the hutong. Evidently, that neighbor nor anyone else whose hands this fish passed through could spare the time, because later in the day, that same fish was returned to Heidi via a different neighbor. Regifting is common in China, but your gift usually does not return to you the same day!

Heidi had a boyfriend, Guo YiSheng, who was a gifted oil painter. They had attended the same high school but parted when she left for Beijing and he to Jiangsu Normal University to study art. A few months after accepting Jesus, Heidi decided to visit Guo and take him a Bible. The seeds were planted, and later Heidi led him to the Lord.

The following year, Guo graduated and was assigned a teaching position in a school far from Beijing. It was a brand-new facility, and after a few years of teaching, he would also have been given a new apartment. It was a great opportunity and seemed perfect for the newly married couple.

However, Heidi's dream was still to live in Beijing. You may have heard the saying *happy wife, happy life,* so after a year of teaching, Guo gave up his position and moved to Beijing. It certainly was a leap of faith. But God met them and provided Guo with a job illustrating educational materials, and Heidi worked for Will Go as our secretary-bookkeeper.

The Guo family with "little" Ollie.

They both continued to grow in God, attending our fellowship each Sunday.

When they were expecting their first child, the doctor told them, "Because of your bleeding, this baby may have numerous birth defects. I recommend you abort as soon as possible." This was not news Heidi and Guo expected to hear. They were devastated and came to us. We listened and empathized with them.

Quietly, Larry said, "It's a life."

Immediately, Guo responded, "Yes. This is our baby, perfect or not. He's ours."

We prayed together and asked God for a miracle. In summer 2001, their little boy, JiYuan, was born perfect. We thanked God for answering our prayers. A few months later, he joined his parents for his first Fellowship Christmas party. We all affectionately call him Ollie, short for Olympic because he was born the year that Beijing received the bid for the 2008 Summer Olympics. Today, he studies art and is the illustration artist for this book. Certainly, God works miracles from potentially tragic circumstances. Ollie told us himself, "God saved me twice; once for life on earth and again for life in heaven." We are all grateful.

We Buy Our Own Apartment

We continued to live and work in China on our student visas, which included the hotel dorm room housing. With several students coming regularly to study the Bible, we needed more space and privacy, so we rented a nearby apartment. However, we found this was illegal, not for us but for the landlord. So after collecting several months' rent—which was a substantial income at that time in Beijing—we were asked to leave. As we lamented our circumstances, David (the Burden Bearer), who by now had become a trusted friend, suggested we buy our own apartment. This seemed like a good idea, but we needed to hear from God. We prayed.

A few weeks later, David asked us to visit the construction site of a new apartment complex in northern Beijing. As we walked through the management office door, a peace settled in our hearts. It was time to buy our own apartment.

About six months later, we arrived at the management office to pick up the Red Book, proof of full payment for our apartment. Since it was still illegal for foreigners to own property in China, we had planned to put David's name on the title deed. However, the property manager assured us that government policies were changing soon, and we should put our name on the document. Larry Dean Johnson was officially stamped on the deed. We nearly danced back to our car with our precious Red Book in hand, planning to celebrate with a platter of Jing jiang roezi (Beijing soy sauce over shredded pork loin). David, on the other hand, looked worried. In a somber tone, he warned, "Don't ever lose your Red Book." Perhaps God had given him a premonition of things to come.

The apartment shell was done; now it was our turn to go to work. In 1998 Beijing, you had to buy the windows, doors, and kitchen and bathroom fixtures yourselves and arrange their installation. Michael, one of the first young men to accept the Lord and join our fellowship, volunteered to help.

We arrived at a gigantic construction market and picked out windows for the whole apartment. We were quite happy with the price. Unknown to us, the seller called Michael over and gave him a kickback of 1500 RMB (Renminbi, the official currency of China). At that time, it was the equivalent of about three months' salary. Michael, who had recently lost his job, immediately came to us and insisted we take the money.

Living with the people—our Chinese apartment.

"It's not my money," he stated as he smilingly pressed the bundle of cash into Larry's hand.

God never forgets. Michael's integrity and willingness to serve others has helped him grow a successful business in China today.

> Is not your reverence your confidence? And the integrity of your ways your hope? (Job 4:6)

> The integrity of the upright will guide them, but the perversity of the unfaithful will destroy them. (Proverbs 11:3)

Miracle in Gansu

Evangelism is always at the forefront of my (Larry) heart, so when Adrian (my Beijing classmate and coleader of our fellowship) asked me to join him on a ministry trip to Gansu, I packed my bag. It would be Adrian's third visit, having already established a relationship with the monks of this remote Buddhist Monastery. Gansu is over fourteen hundred kilometers (895 miles) from Beijing, and the high-speed trains of today's China were still on the drawing board. We had already traveled for twenty-four hours and still had two hours to our first destination. Finally, we pulled into the Lanzhou depot and debarked with our plastic multistriped bags packed with supplies the monks had requested.

We managed to get to the bus station for the last leg of our journey and found our seats. In those days, the bus didn't move until every seat was occupied. Slowly, the bus filled, and finally, it seemed we would take off. But just before the driver closed the door, twenty kids piled into the bus, sitting anywhere and everywhere. The aisles were impassable.

That's not all that was impassable. Curve after curve over narrow muddy roads, gouged with deep potholes, left us feeling like we were riding a Tilt-A-Whirl at the county fair. Our driver didn't seem fazed as he pushed ahead like an Indy race car driver. And then someone tapped my shoulder and asked me to pass "the bag" to a boy who looked like he couldn't get it fast enough. The clear plastic bag was already brimming with the stomach contents of many sick kids. I gingerly passed it forward, praying I wouldn't have to use it! With the bus still careening over the road, a more seasoned passenger opened the window and emptied it. I continued to pray.

After nearly two days of travel, we arrived at the monastery. The monks warmly welcomed us and gave us some much-appreciated soothing tea. After presenting the gifts—educational supplies and assorted health products—we began to share Jesus. Before leaving for the night, we asked if we could pray with them. A middle-aged monk slowly made his way toward us. He was bent nearly half over and suffered severe pain.

As we laid hands on him and began praying in tongues, he began to raise up, slowly at first. But as we continued to call on the name of Jesus, the monk stood straight up, pain free. There was such rejoicing. We told them it was Jesus, the King of Kings and Lord of Lords, who healed this man. "Why else would God bring us to you?" Adrian asked. "God himself arranged this divine appointment." Every monk in that place prayed to ask Jesus into their lives. What a mighty God we serve.

The physical journey home wasn't much different, but as I passed "the bag," I could still see the joyous expression on that monk's face, our new brother totally healed and praising God. I rejoiced over more new souls in the kingdom. It was worth it all.

Midnight Baptism

We were considering places for our fellowship baptism. Someone suggested Miyun Reservoir, the largest artificial lake in Asia. It was built by the hands of migrant laborers and area farmers. Though initially it did not hold water, it now served as a major water source for many of Beijing's twenty million residents. We booked several hotel rooms near there, packed picnic lunches, and carpooled to the area. Beforehand, Larry, Adrian, and Michael had checked out the reservoir and found it ideal. People could walk down a few stairsteps and be at the water's edge. We were all set, or so we thought.

Because we did not want to call attention to ourselves, we planned the baptism at midnight. After a wonderful time of praise and worship, the Word, and prayer, we began our hike down to the reservoir.

We couldn't believe our eyes. Where were the stairs down to the reservoir?

We had not taken into consideration that Beijing engineers had programmed the spillways to open and refill the reservoir during the night. The water level had risen three feet since the guys' earlier visit. Undeterred, with God's canopy of stars lighting our way, we joined hands and entered the water. One by one, each baptism was completed. To this day, it remains as one of our most memorable nights in China, not solely for the baptisms but for His powerful presence, provision, and protection. Only God.

Stamp, Stamp, Stamp

We had returned to the States to update supporters on our work in China and were excited to return home to Beijing. Our passports had been sent to a Washington, DC, visa agency to renew our Chinese visa. Only two weeks remained before departure,

A baptism at midnight—Larry, Adrian, and Michael check it out.

but our passports had not been returned. We called UPS, who tracked them to a specific depot and confirmed they had not gone any further. "Please make a clean sweep of the facility," Larry implored. "We have to have them in two weeks." UPS told us not to worry and expedited both new passports and visas. The new passports were beautiful. Instead of the usual generic pages with a light blue background, these new pages were embossed with different state seals, including Iowa. This seemingly inconsequential detail would have a big impact in the coming months.

Up until this point, we had been operating with a visitor visa which expired every six months. That's when God dropped in our hearts to register Will Go Inc. not as a nonprofit but as a representative USA consultant company in China. We gathered the applicable government forms and set to work. After a few months' work, checking and rechecking, we submitted our documents to the proper Chinese agency. They were immediately returned to us. The accompanying letter informed us that we needed the Iowa seal on our documents. It seemed impossible until God spoke to Larry's heart and said, *Look in your passport.* And you may remember that our new passports included a seal of our state, Iowa. For the next several days, Larry painstakingly copied, cut out tiny pieces of numbers and letters and assembled an amazing Iowa seal. We photocopied the title page with "our" beautiful seal and resubmitted the application.

About one month later, we received notice for our personal interview, the last step in ratifying our representative business status in China. We nervously stood in front of three government officers as they solemnly studied our application papers and peppered us with questions: Why did you come to China? What are you doing here? How long will you stay? What's your purpose? Their unsmiling expressions never changed.

Miracle passports—the Iowa seal.

Finally, Larry said to our translator, "Should I just tell the truth?"

With a look of astonishment, she simply replied, "I'm here to translate."

Taking a deep breath, Larry quietly said, "We are Christians, and we came to help."

They looked at each other, at us, and then *stamp, stamp, stamp*. It was official. We were Will Go USA Representative Office, Beijing.

Will Go is translated *neng zuo* in Chinese and means "can do." Our prayer was to live up to the name God had given our mission organization.

The White Paper Flower

We had just returned home when we noticed a large white paper flower on a pole at the entrance of our neighbor's home. This signaled a death in the family. We soon learned that their beloved wife and mother had died. Larry, knowing they had a big family, bought a case of Coca-Cola, Dove candy bars, and fruit and went down to sit with them during their Chinese wake. They never forgot it. This small act of kindness had a big payoff, which we will share later in our story.

Rescuing the Unloved: Living Tree Orphanage

While working in China, God helped us bring love and hope to several groups of people. One of those groups were children with cerebral palsy living in an orphanage founded by Ms. Wang. God divinely interrupted this fast-rising star of the Communist Party for His plans and purposes. Her story still brings tears to our eyes:

It was a cool fall day as Ms. Wang arrived early for her meeting with government officials. They were to discuss implementation of new social reforms in China, and she, a respected comrade, had been hand-picked for this new project. As she proceeded toward the meeting room, she could hear a faint whimpering, then silence, then more whimpering. This was an old brick office building; who or what could be making such distressed sounds? She felt compelled to find out and followed the sound up the stairwell to the top floor. As she opened the door, she was shocked to see a lone baby girl lying naked on the cement floor. Immediately, her heart went out to the child, and she pledged to help.

Ms. Wang soon learned that many disabled babies were left in such circumstances to die. Though she had only recently received Christ as her Savior, she felt God was asking her to rescue these little ones. From this God-chance encounter, she began Living Tree Orphanage for cerebral palsy children. Severe push-back came from her parents and friends, all high-ranking government bureaucrats, who could not understand her ignoring a prestigious job for such humanity. But she steadfastly pushed through.

God sent her many partners for the work, including us. Will Go (our company in China) coordinated special outings for the children. One of our favorite events was to take twenty-six of them, with their wheelchairs, and their caregivers by chartered bus to the Beijing Zoo. We will never forget the smiles and joy of that day. Now, some thirty years later, Will Go continues to help, recently painting beautiful pictures for the walls of their new location. God's love never fails.

Love and Light Orphanage

We also partnered with another orphanage called Love and Light, a work born from profound tragedy. As Brother Li and his wife humbly recounted the events that would become the catalyst for this orphanage, Larry said the words God had spoken to him years before resounded in his heart: *What could you say you have done for me?* Their testimony challenged us to again reexamine our own lives, motives, and actions. We have taken the liberty to title their testimony "From Ashes to Life."

Brother Li said he was called to preach in his late teens and traveled on foot from village to village sharing Jesus with small underground house churches. His offerings were meager, often only a little food for himself. Despite the hardships, he met Cai, a sweet Christian sister, who became his wife. Within a year, they had a little baby boy.

Even so, Brother Li (now Pastor Li) continued his ministry to underground village churches, leaving his wife and small son at home alone for long stretches of time. They, too, suffered abject poverty, coupled with feelings of loneliness and neglect. Early one morning, unable to face another day, Cai decided to end her life and that of her son. She set herself and their house on fire. Thankfully, a neighbor heard the cries of the child and came running, pulling the little boy from the flames. He was saved from serious harm, but not his mother, whose clothes were ablaze. Though her face, arms, and upper body were mercilessly burned, she miraculously survived.

Word was sent to Cai's husband, who immediately returned home. "When I saw the misery of my wife and little son, I threw myself on the mercy of the Lord," he said, "and repented for my insensitivity and grave lack of care for my family. And now we, too, were homeless." A few days later, standing among the ashes of his former home, Pastor Li prayed for God's grace and guidance. "God reminded me of the many others I had met on the road who were abandoned and without hope. He assured me that He wanted to provide for them and us." Plans were formulated and shared with Christian brothers and sisters across China.

Within a short time, they opened Love and Light Orphanage, a home near Beijing for orphans and others discarded by family. Within a few years, eighty children from all over China were sent to them. God raised up partners from all over the world, and we were among them.

Will Go Consultant Company, China, initiated art camps and health education. Will Go teams brought school supplies, clothing, and even teddy bears. But most importantly, the love of God was demonstrated and His Word preached daily. Many of those children are scattered throughout China, living healthy and productive lives. God is an awesome God.

> He helps orphans and widows, and he loves foreigners and gives them food and clothes. (Deuteronomy 10:18 NCV)

God Opens the Geriatric Field

On Sunday mornings, we attended Beijing International Christian Fellowship (BICF), allowed by the Chinese government for foreigners. Anne, a tall, dark-haired British lady, frequently sat near us. One Sunday, she invited us to visit Song Tang, a newly opened elderly care home. Enthusiastically, we said yes.

Anne introduced us to Dr. Li Wei, founder and director of Song Tang Elderly Care Home. This kind-hearted man with a keen business sense could foresee that China was entering a new era, due in part to the One Child Law, implemented in 1980. Many adult children, unable to care for senior members of their family, were looking for alternatives. Nursing home care became a necessity. Though conditions at

Song Tang were tough by Western standards, it provided a bed, food, and twenty-four-hour care. The home quickly grew to over one hundred elders.

Dr. Li Wei had an open heart to God and foreign Christians. We were allowed to freely share the Bible, and thankfully, many elders received Jesus as their Savior. But to be honest, this was a hard ministry. His first nursing home was far from us, and conditions were harsh. Elders, with their caregiver, lived in small, dimly lit rooms. Winters were even more difficult. Everyone was layered in heavy cotton-padded clothing (resembling a Canadian goalie) and could barely move. Each week, we faithfully went door to door, asking the elder and caregiver if we could visit. Over time, relationships were built, and we had a small Bible study there.

Operating such a facility was expensive, and fees paid by the families did not cover all the costs. To keep things running, Dr. Li Wei sold many of his family antiques. His pretty wife, who worked in the movie industry, also helped with funding. One of our projects was to buy several washing machines to relieve the caregivers. They were washing the elders' clothing and bedding, all by hand, outside—even in winter.

I wish we had pictures. Early on a bright sunny morning, we joined an army of Beijing volunteers who provided their own cars and vans to physically move all the elders and staff to the new Song Tang facility. We resembled a large locomotive train, backing up to attach another car. One by one, each vehicle was loaded and moved into the queue. When the final car was filled, we snaked in unison down the highway to Song Tang's new destination. This move was not by choice; the government was constructing a new road right through the property.

Dr. Li Wei's second location had ward-type rooms with eight to ten elders per room. One bed was designated for the caregiver, who also lived in the room and was responsible to dress, feed, toilet, and change bedding for all "her" people, twenty-four seven. It was very tough work.

Many of the caregivers were young girls from the countryside lured to Beijing with the promise of earning real money. Though Dr. Li Wei's job came with room and board, the work was too difficult for some, and they chose to run away. However, finding the bus station on foot proved daunting, and most ended up at the police station, forcing Dr. Li Wei to retrieve them. There were heartache and tears on both sides. Though it sounds like a cliché, Jesus was the answer.

December was a major evangelism month. Our Will Go Fellowship spent hours shopping, wrapping, and transporting gifts to Song Tang for all the elders and the one hundred caregivers. The Christmas story was shared, carols sung, and salvation presented. Dr. Li Wei told us that everyone looked forward to our big Christmas party because it was such an encouragement. Today, Song Tang, now with hospital accreditation, resides in a modern building with a beautiful courtyard. Recently, Larry asked if there was anything else we could do for them. Li Wei's answer? "Don't forget us at Christmastime."

In 2016, we revisited Song Tang with a team from Canada. Immediately, one of the caregivers came running to us. "Remember me? I was one of the first caregivers here, and you told me about Jesus." What a sweet reunion. We pray this will be repeated many times in heaven.

> So shall My word be that goes forth from My mouth;
> It shall not return to Me void,
> But it shall accomplish what I please,
> And it shall prosper in the thing for which I sent it.
> (Isaiah 55:11)

"Remember me? You told me about Jesus."
Hayley, our granddaughter, joined us from the States.

Mr. and Mrs. Yang

Shawn Bao, grandson of the last emperor of China, introduced us to Mr. and Mrs. Yang, who operated a small countryside elderly care home. Each elder had their own room, were ambulatory, and in fair health. Caregivers again came from the countryside, but unlike Dr. Li Wei's caregivers, they each had their own room. Mrs. Yang supervised the care, and their son cooked for everyone. It really was a family affair.

Again, our main heart was to introduce people to Jesus, so during our introductory meeting, Larry asked if he could share some Bible verses. We were a bit surprised after reading John 3:1–17 and explaining the meaning of "you must be born again," that they immediately wanted to ask Jesus into their hearts. Later we learned that, as children, they had heard many Bible stories. The seeds had already been planted, and we were the privileged harvesters. Shortly after that, we began having regular church services in their home.

The church service was also open to local villagers. Unfortunately, one of those villagers was not happy to hear the gospel preached. She'd come to the meeting and then, about halfway through, leave and report us to the police. It was still illegal for foreigners to preach to Chinese. However, during that season in China, the government was taking a one-eye-open, one-eye-closed stance. If you were doing enough good, they winked their eye. Mr. Yang had shown county officials the improvements we had made to the nursing home—a remodeled stainless-steel kitchen and refurbished dining room. Knowing what we had done, the police really did not want to catch us. Nevertheless, she continued to call, forcing them to do something.

The police knew we usually left around six o'clock but still waited until nine o'clock to make a surprise entry to the home, probably expecting to find everyone sleeping. Unfortunately, Mrs. Yang, though already in bed, was reading the Bible we had given her. Possessing a foreign Bible was still a crime in China, though it wasn't regularly enforced. When the policeman asked her if she was reading a foreign Bible, she truthfully answered yes.

Immediately, they told her, "We must confiscate it; you are not allowed to own this foreign book."

She later recounted that night: "I took a deep breath and strengthened myself. 'Please, let me remove the markers from my favorite verses,' she pleaded, 'then you can take my Bible.' Slowly . . . one . . . two . . . three—I had more than twenty to remove." Finally, the police became very impatient and told her to keep the Bible and left. She was overjoyed and thanked God for preserving the Word for her.

We decided to discontinue church services for a few months so as not to bring trouble to Mr. and Mrs. Yang. But eventually they asked us to return, saying so many missed the worship and Word. We never saw that lady again nor did the police investigate any further. A few years later, new road construction also forced the closing of their home.

During this time, we contemplated opening our own nursing home. Mr. Yang introduced us to an influential man in the central government who cordially told us we had come "too high," meaning we did not have the monetary investment required at that level of government. "The appointment after yours will be with the United States Red Cross, who will be investing one million dollars into China. You need to meet with officials on the county level," he said. He wrote down our names and sincerely thanked us for the renovations at Mr. Yang's nursing home. We later wondered if he was responsible for the government contacting us to do to the BTV television program for elders.

We took his advice and began meeting with people willing to sell their properties in the countryside around Beijing. But it seemed family members could never agree on a price. After several attempts with different pieces of property, we concluded that God did not want us to open our own nursing home but that geriatric training was the real need. We began praying into that vision.

Like a Puzzle, One Piece at a Time

God sees the whole picture, but we do not. However, as we walk by faith, the pieces drop into place. Heidi had been translating for us at Mr. Yang's and Dr. Li Wei's homes. Her gentle and kind ways had won the hearts of the directors and elders alike. We really relied on her. But then, shortly after her marriage to Guo, she told us she was pregnant and could no longer work. We were happy for them but wondered how we would manage without her. We should have known God had it covered.

God Sends Sarah

We met Albert Lou, a devout Christian brother and New York businessman at the BICF (church). He had opened six A&W restaurants in Beijing and approached us to teach conversational English. We had been praying for another evangelistic opportunity, so this was perfect. Twice a week, we taught on various subjects, answered questions, and shared Jesus. Albert provided free root beer floats and hamburgers, a "taste of home" bonus. But our greatest reward was seeing so many people come to the Lord. Our fellowship grew. And God, in his sovereignty, was ordering our next footsteps.

Sarah (Liu HongLin), the secretary and assistant manager for the A&W franchises, also attended our English classes. At the close of every class, she would boldly say, "Larry, I want to work for Will Go." We dismissed it because we knew her salary at A&W was much higher than we could ever pay. However, she remained persistent, even showing up at our apartment with a signed contract she had made herself! She stated she would work for free. "My husband is very wealthy—no problem." We were amazed at the provision of God even when we kept trying to shut the door. He knew we needed her!

Sarah was also a nurse—confident, outgoing, and highly educated. She had been chosen by the Chinese government for advanced medical training in Singapore so she could train other nurses (how much more perfect could it get?). She immediately grasped the idea of geriatric training and began recruiting nursing home directors and their caregivers to join our upcoming seminars.

At the same time, we returned to the States to recruit volunteers to help plan, prepare, and execute this God-inspired vision. Pastor Dennis Nonnemacher, from Wisconsin, was the first to get onboard and flew to Beijing with Connie, a sweet nurse from his congregation. Together, we chose and compiled the materials for our caregiver training. And again, Joel Holm (remember, he had introduced David) volunteered his Chinese translator, Linda, a gifted young lady living in Beijing. After several weeks of hard work, we were ready. We were so excited to hold our first Will Go Geriatric Training Seminar.

The First Training
The first training was held with Dr. Li Wei's managers and caregivers. Complete books with all the fifteen talks and thirty

Sarah—Chinese nurse crucial to the launching and success of our
Will Go Geriatric Seminars.

skills were given to each student. Our seminars, intended to improve the well-being of resident elders, quickly caught on, and we found ourselves in multiple facilities all over China. Testimonies poured in too, the impact greater than we ever imagined. After the talk on preventing decubitus (bedsores) and the skill on repositioning bedfast patients, one home initiated a system of bells that rang every two hours, reminding the caregiver to turn their patient. Decubitus sores were greatly reduced. Another home reported saving a lady's life with the Heimlich maneuver skill; the week before, an elder had choked to death on a sticky rice ball. The communication talk gave caregivers practical ways to help deaf, blind, lonely, or agitated elders. Many homes reported a difference in accidents and general contentment of their residents.

We were so thankful for the physical improvements but were also concerned about their spiritual well-being. Our forty-hour seminars included a talk on care of the dying. After this solemn talk, Larry reminded everyone, "We will all face death." He carefully outlined the choice all humankind has because of Jesus's atonement on the cross. "We can begin a new life of peace with God today. Confess your sins to Him and by faith acknowledge what Jesus has done for you. God will hear your prayer and make a home for you in heaven."

When Larry asked how many wanted to accept what Jesus had done for them, nearly everyone raised their hand. Of course, God knows the heart, but seeds were planted. Some nursing homes even asked if their elders could hear Larry's salvation message, convicting the hearts of elders who were seventy, eighty, and ninety years old, bringing them to God.

Our mission's goal to help improve the lives of people and introduce them to Jesus was being met. God continued to supply wonderful nurses from the USA, Australia, and

Seminars were held in multiple provinces.

Government leaders were sometimes required to attend our seminars.

A grand party with certificates and cake culminated every training.

Nurses from around the world came to teach (Heather Johnson).

from within China. And because of the generosity of our donors, all geriatric seminars were given free of charge. Larry and I were even invited to the Great Hall of the People to receive recognition for our role in helping the elderly of China. Amazing. Only God.

> Then he told them many things in parables, saying: "A farmer went out to sow his seed. As he was scattering the seed, some fell along the path, and the birds came and ate it up. Some fell on rocky places, where it did not have much soil. It sprang up quickly, because the soil was shallow. But when the sun came up, the plants were scorched, and they withered because they had no root. Other seed fell among thorns, which grew up and choked the plants. Still other seed fell on good soil, where it produced a crop—a hundred, sixty or thirty times what was sown. Whoever has ears, let them hear." (Matthew 13:3–9 NIV)

A $7,000 Taxi

One of the nurses who came to help us in China was Mrs. Anne Abbott, a lady in her seventies. We were speaking at Pastor Wayne Wachsmuth's church on Harlem Avenue in Chicago, and although we did not know her, the Holy Spirit picked her out of the congregation. Larry looked directly at her and said, "You should come to China and help us." After the service Mrs. Abbott explained she was a registered nurse and would love to do something for God. She signed up for the next seminar team. Just two weeks before she was to arrive in Beijing, she contacted us to inquire how we would be traveling around Beijing.

Our JinBei (Golden Cup) van was used to bless many people.

Larry told her that we rented taxis, to which she replied, "I don't like taxis."

He told her that we didn't really have a choice since we hadn't yet saved enough money to buy a van.

"How much more do you need?" she asked.

When Larry told her we had $7,000, but needed another $7,000, she replied, "It will be in your bank tomorrow. I really do not want to ride in a taxi."

> And my God shall supply all your need according to
> His riches in glory by Christ Jesus. (Philippians 4:19)

Red Book Lost

Larry and Sarah scrambled to get the van bought, paperwork completed, and license plates on before Anne arrived. It meant flagging taxis and running from one office to another. One agency had asked to inspect our Red Book—for what reason, we were never sure—but the precious Red Book was with them. Until it was not. Had it been left in a taxi or on a counter? Our only hope was that whoever found it would return it.

Within twenty-four hours, we received a phone call with explicit instructions to meet under one of Beijing's viaducts with $1,500 USD in exchange for our Red Book. Larry and Sarah (who adamantly volunteered to assist) arrived at the appointed time, but no one showed. A second call came, still demanding $1,500 USD. Exasperated, Larry replied, "I'll give you $300 USD." The caller hung up. We never heard from him again nor did we ever see our Red Book.

Despite this unsettling event, God seemed to say, *I've got this; don't worry.* And as you will read later, God again worked miraculously on our behalf.

Four days later, we picked up Anne in her new taxi-van. She happily sat in the front seat, taking in all the sights. That van carted us to numerous geriatric seminars, brought people to our fellowship, and took all kinds of goods and supplies to multiple outreaches. It was a great blessing long after Anne's return to Chicago.

Sarah Leaves

The train had just pulled away from the depot, and we were settled into our soft sleeper when Sarah knocked on the door. "I wanted to talk to you even before the seminar started but thought it best to wait until we finished." she said. "I love working for you and living in Beijing. You are my friends, and I don't want to stop working for Will Go." But Wang Pan, her husband, was requesting she return home very soon. He missed his wife and never imagined that her desire to work in Beijing was more than a whim. He thought it would have dissipated long ago, but instead, years had passed.

It was no secret that we relied on Sarah considerably. She had jump-started our geriatric seminars, and her expert communication and confidence opened many doors. Larry encouraged her that the right thing to do was to honor her husband and their marriage. As difficult as it was to say goodbye to Sarah, we knew that God would again provide for the next steps in our work.

> Who can find a virtuous wife?
> For her worth is far above rubies.
> The heart of her husband safely trusts her
> So he will have no lack of gain.
> She does him good and not evil,
> All the days of her life.
> (Proverbs 31:10–12)

Heidi Returns

By now, little Ollie was walking, and Heidi's mother-in-law lived with them full-time to help with his care. She and Guo were faithful in our fellowship. One Sunday, Heidi said to us, "I'd like to come back to work. Could you give me the geriatric materials to study? Let me try." She did an awesome job. What's more, we were moving into a more evangelistic season, and Heidi's love for God came shining through. She fearlessly translated in many different situations and places. Little did we know how needed she would be at our next seminar in Bai HaiDe County. But just a week before we were to leave, we had a surprise.

Thieves

We were excited to get to the office and complete our preparations for our upcoming Bai HaiDe seminar. It was a beautiful blue-sky day in Beijing, a pleasant welcome after several days of smog. Summer roses adorned the highway as we drove the usual thirty minutes to our sturdy, Russian-built office building on the third ring road (the third highway belt of seven encircling Beijing). It was Monday morning.

We were speechless. As soon as Larry unlocked the door, we could see our office was a mess. Both computers were gone as well as the video camera and other items purchased for our upcoming seminar. After regaining our composure, we sat down and called the police. At least the thieves left the office chairs.

The police arrived and took a complete report, promising to do their best to locate our missing items. Much to our surprise, they showed up a few days later with our Gateway computer and video camera. They apologized for not finding our Toshiba computer but said it was too common and popular in China to track. As soon as they left, Larry opened the video camera case and was shocked to see several pieces of jewelry, watches, and rings in the bottom compartment.

That afternoon, Larry returned the stolen items to the police station. "You saved us so much trouble," the officer said. "You can't imagine how serious it is for stolen property to go missing." He thanked Larry profusely, explaining all missing items had to be accounted for and that the officers involved could be demoted and required to pay retribution. God's grace spared them. It was a good day.

Training County Leaders in Bai HaiDe

We were excited for the opportunity to train these young county leaders who oversaw numerous homes and literally influenced the care of hundreds of elders. However, it was apparent they felt a caregiver seminar was below their position and reluctantly participated. Our first three days were uncomfortable, and now it was Thursday, our gospel day. After the death and dying talk, Larry usually presented a salvation message, but knowing they were government employees and probably Communist Party members, we struggled whether we should proceed or not. Though we had found "freedom" in China to evangelize, it was still illegal. It might mean the canceling of our seminars or, worse, an early invitation to leave China. We needed to hear from God and give Heidi the privilege to decline to translate. After a night of prayer, we all felt peace to go ahead, though with a slightly different format.

Larry shared the gospel but this time did not ask for a public commitment. Instead, he said, "If you want to know more about God's plan for you, please come forward and take one of these booklets." Our most hostile leader was the first to rush forward and pick one up. Everyone followed suit.

The next day was unbelievable. The attitude of this man and the other leaders had completely changed, reflected by their enthusiastic participation in our final testing. Our graduation cake (served after every seminar) never tasted so sweet.

Side note: One thousand colorful, high-quality, glossy-covered booklets detailing God's plan for humankind from Genesis to Revelation were miraculously flown into Beijing. Every time Brad, a brother from Burlington, Iowa, flew his boss from Macao to China, he loaded these booklets in his bag and delivered them to us. This timely gift was the perfect tool for China's emerging educated leaders such as the Bai HaiDe County men. Only God.

The Barefoot Doctor
Let us introduce Dr. Ma, one of China's heroes in the faith. This lady, in her mid-seventies, operated a care home for forty people. She provided food, shelter, and clothing not only for elders but also for many crippled, poor, and homeless, trusting only God to provide. Most remarkable was the family setting she created for this eclectic group of souls. One former beggar, who had existed under a Beijing bridge for years, said with a big smile, "This is my first family." God's Word was preached regularly and practiced daily. When we asked how she came to operate this home, she told us her remarkable story.

Everything had changed in 1966. It was the beginning of Chairman Mao's purge known as the Cultural Revolution. "Because of my status as a doctor, I became an automatic enemy of the state," she said. For her "crime," she was sent to a remote area in southern China, where she labored in the fields and served the villages as a doctor. When her shoes wore out, they were not replaced; hence, she was known as *the barefoot doctor*. Severe hunger and poverty were the norm.

Days turned into months, and months into years—ten of them. Dr. Ma began to experience digestive issues and abdominal pain. She was diagnosed with colon cancer. "Because you have been such a good comrade," her leaders told her, "we will send you back to Beijing to die."

As the slow northbound train headed for Beijing, she had time to reflect on her life. She said she was so sorry that in ten years time, she had never uttered God's name or the name of Jesus. She remorsefully begged God for forgiveness and pledged to serve Him with whatever days she had left. The government had reopened one church, so the following Sunday, still suffering great abdominal pain, she went. She told the pastor she was dying and wanted to do something for God. "I can't go to heaven empty-handed," she said. "Please, give me a chance to serve Him." Reluctantly, he gave her a list of elders who were also sick and told her to go and pray for them.

In those days, most people lived in six-floor apartment buildings with no elevator. Dr. Ma said it took fortitude and every bit of energy to get out of bed, travel by bus to different locations in Beijing, climb the multiple flights of stairs, and finally pray with a suffering, lonely elder. After two weeks, she had exhausted her list. So she went back to the pastor and asked for another list. After the first month, she was amazed that she was still alive, and the pain had diminished. The second month, she realized that she felt better and was getting stronger. After the third month, she felt fine and went back to the doctor to check her status. The doctor said, "I can't explain it, but you are cancer free."

Dr. Ma testified, "As I went, God healed me."

But for you who revere my name, the sun of righteousness will rise with healing in its rays. And

you will go out and frolic like well-fed calves.
(Malachi 4:2 NIV)

As she continued her prayer ministry to the elders, she began to see how much they suffered from isolation and loneliness. God began formulating a plan in her heart. Though she was seventy years old, she decided to open a nursing home "so the lonely could be together."

But of course, such an endeavor costs money. Dr. Ma sent out a plea to many different house churches and brothers and sisters across China. One day a sister arrived, wearing oversized pants and a coat. Dr. Ma said she dipped into this pocket and that one, unbuttoned more pockets, and continued to bring out stacks of RMB (the official currency of China), all for the cause of the new home. It was a great encouragement.

However, a month later, she still did not have the final 10,000 RMB needed to finish the setup. She pleaded with God to touch hearts and bring in the funds. But then a still small voice spoke to her and said, "Dr. Ma, what about your bank account? You have 10,000 RMB." She tried arguing with God. That was all money she had. But her heart was convicted. She took the leap of faith and withdrew the funds. Her journey in nursing home care had begun.

And He looked up and saw the rich putting their gifts into the treasury, and He saw also a certain poor widow putting in two mites. So He said, "Truly I say to you that this poor widow has put in more than all; for all these out of their abundance have put in offerings for God, but she out of her poverty put in all the livelihood that she had." (Luke 21:1–4)

Will Go became one of several partners that helped Dr. Ma continue the work. One morning Larry woke up and said, "God spoke to my heart during the night to take 2,400 RMB to Dr. Ma today." It was still morning when we arrived.

After counting the money, Dr. Ma looked up with tears in her eyes and said, "This is the exact amount I needed to pay our rent today."

I will bless the Lord who has given me counsel; my heart also instructs me in the night seasons. (Psalm 16:7)

Dr. Ma sent all her caregivers to our geriatric seminars with visible improvements of care for their residents. She remained our friend long after the work had been passed on to others.

Short Reflections on Other Nursing Homes

Because of our geriatric training, we made strong connections with many different homes:

Feng Tai Government Home

This home had more than five hundred elders and hundreds of staff. Will Go was able to purchase Christmas gifts for everyone and present the Christmas story in Word and song two years in a row. They openly welcomed the gospel.

Northern Beijing Government Home

This was the cleanest and most organized of all the homes we visited. All staff was hired from the community and worked in shifts. The manager himself was on dialysis and knew the power of cleanliness. He had his own bathroom.

Hebei Province Home

We had finished another weeklong seminar, but before we left, Larry asked the manager if he could give a short message to the elders. She agreed, and everyone was assembled in the commons area. About halfway through the service, a uniformed policeman stepped into the room. Larry said a lump rose in his throat, and he considered cutting it short. But as he looked at the elders, he thought they deserved to hear God's Word. He proceeded, ending with a salvation message. When he finished, the policeman walked up to him and said, "My mother lives here and is a Christian. She seldom gets to hear any preaching. Thank you."

Anhui Government Home for Single Men

Our love for elders took us many places, this time far from Beijing to a countryside home in the province of Anhui. We visited individually with many men in this sparse place, sharing Jesus. It was extremely hot, so we had the idea to buy a standing fan for each man's room. We purchased thirty fans at the local store and arranged to have them transported to the home. However, we later learned that the government was there to confiscate the fans.

What a disappointment. In retrospect, we should have checked with upper leaders to see what gift would be best for the men. The home was completely free for men without families. Was electricity for thirty fans too expensive? Or perhaps the men did not want a breeze blowing directly on them? Whatever the reason—lesson learned.

Hao De Nursing Home

Though this home was about one hour outside Beijing, we frequently visited with programs, Bible stories, and various helps. Sun YuFang, a wonderful, caring lady had accepted the Lord and wanted her residents to know Him too.

A Home for Lepers

"They seldom get visitors," the pastor said. "Many people are still afraid of lepers. But I think they would love to hear your message. Will you go?"

Larry and Heidi preach the good news.

We quickly bought bags of rice, towels, and soap and joined him for a trek through multiple fields of corn. If our lives depended on it, we could never find that place again. Our small yellow cab could barely keep on the path, meant more for a bicycle than a car. Some forty-five minutes later, we arrived at the leper colony where about twenty-five people made their home.

This remote home was started in the 1950s by a German missionary, who for ten years was their sole provider, bringing food, clothing, and medicine regularly. However, during the political unrest of the sixties, he faced expulsion from China. Unwilling to leave his precious leprous friends to starve, he contacted the nearby Three-Self Church of China. Though they, too, endured much persecution, they never abandoned the colony.

We were welcomed with open arms, and everyone seemed overjoyed to hear Larry's message. We prayed with them and gave our gifts, but the gift we received no money could buy. Their witness of peace and joy in the face of extreme hardship changed our lives. They were living epistles of the words in Hebrews:

> Don't be obsessed with getting more material things. Be relaxed with what you have. Since God assured us, "I'll never let you down, never walk off and leave you," we can boldly quote,
>
> God is there, ready to help,
> I'm fearless no matter what.
> Who or what can get to me?
> (Hebrews 13:5–6 MSG)

Helping Hands Partnership

This story reflects the supreme intervention of God in our everyday lives. After church (BICF, Beijing), we decided to grab some lunch at a nearby A&W. We had just picked up our food when we noticed a team of Americans. Though we didn't usually make a habit of introducing ourselves to strangers, we felt led to greet them. Amazingly, a mutual friend had given them our contact information, but they had lost it and were discussing what to do with the supplies they had brought for us. And then we appeared!

From that divine meeting, Bo and Bonnie Boehning, of Helping Hands Worldwide, have helped Will Go reach thousands of souls, traveling with us also to Africa, Vietnam, and Cuba. Only God.

One Hundred Steps

One of Larry's early translators for the Will Go Fellowship was a young lady named Helen (Chang YaPing). She was studying medicine in Beijing. All too soon, she graduated and took a job back in her hometown of Kunming in Yunnan Province. The following spring, Helen contacted us asking for help to present the gospel to her family. "I've been trying, but it's not going well," she said. "Please come."

After a 1700-mile (2,735 kilometer) train trip, lasting nearly forty hours (which incidentally would only take eleven hours today in China's new bullet trains), we arrived. Thanks to God and Helen's prayers, many of her family members did accept the Lord. We felt the trip was a success. But God wasn't finished yet.

Just the day before we were to leave, Helen took us to the brand-new Kunming International Horticulture Exposition. We arrived at a set of black wrought iron gates to find them locked and a sign that read "Grand Opening Tomorrow." However, the ticket booth was nearby with a lady working inside. By God's grace, we got her attention and convinced her to let us buy a ticket. That was the first miracle.

Workers were so busy giving last minute touches to their displays that no one seemed to notice us. It was like the Garden of Eden with exhibits from all over the world. A tea house at the top of a long flight of steps caught Larry's eye. But since it was such a climb, I insisted we forget it.

A few hours later, while heading back to the gate to go home, we passed the tea house again. Larry stopped and said, "We must go up there. If you don't want to go, wait here. I will go." That didn't seem like much fun, so we all trekked up the one hundred steps, only to be greeted by two Chinese girls who took one look at us, screamed, and shut the door in our faces. A few minutes later, the door reopened, and another little lady invited us in. It was Li ZhengLan.

Yunnan's Tea Princess
As Yunnan's tea princess, Li ZhengLan had the duty of promoting Yunnan tea around China. But this year was extra special; it was the cusp of the new millennium, and China wanted to showcase their multiple teas to the world. She was responsible to select, explain, and serve tea to her guests while performing an ancient, traditional tea ceremony. We had just finished our third selection of tea when Larry said, "Li ZhengLan, have you ever heard the name of Jesus?" Much to our surprise, she said yes. With no one else in the tearoom (the other two girls had completely disappeared), we were able to spend ample time to explain the Scriptures. As Li ZhenLan prayed to receive Jesus, the sweet presence of God tangibly filled that little teahouse.

We stayed in touch with Li ZhengLan, and soon our first trip to the Wa village was underway. We had traveled the 1,700 miles from Beijing again, and we were ready for the second leg. By seven in the morning, we, Helen, her

Larry and Helen at the Kunming Horticultural Expo.

boyfriend, Jesse, and her parents squeezed into a borrowed Chinese minivan, already crammed with 150 backpacks and school supplies. Jesse, who had just obtained his license, was the designated driver.

It's difficult to paint our harrowing journey. The wet, mountainous roads were steep, winding, and ribbon thin. Jesse struggled to stay in the middle. On our way down one of the switchbacks, the car skidded out of control and stopped precariously near the edge of the mountain. Jesse froze. Larry instructed him to set the emergency brake, and as we prayed for God's intervention, they carefully exchanged places. We sat silently as Larry, painstakingly slow, inched the van back up to safety. We were overjoyed to be sitting in the middle of the road and couldn't contain our tears. God had rescued us! Finally, with grateful hearts, we cautiously continued our journey.

Though the roads were terrible, the resplendent beauty of the countryside was breathtaking. Multiple terraces of tea plants in vibrant blue and green colors covered the mountainsides. The Wa people had been nestled there for thousands of generations, growing and picking tea by hand. Many still lived in thatched-roof homes and cooked outdoors.

As we pulled into the village, many beautiful children stood smiling and waving from orderly lines in the school courtyard. Their headmaster, Tian Qiang, had already called the assembly. We inquired if we could tell the children about Jesus, and he said yes. Larry explained that God had arranged this special day for them, bringing us all the way around the world to let them know how much God loved them. He told them how they could accept God's salvation plan for their lives. "When your time is finished here on earth, God has prepared a place for you in heaven. Ask Jesus into your heart," he implored.

Many villagers listened too. Seeds were planted. Then each child received their gift—a backpack filled with school supplies. Tian Qiang was happy too. He believed having their own backpack and supplies would encourage them to attend school more regularly.

The government, also to improve education for the children, had built a beautiful new school. However, it was nearly impossible to keep teachers because of the extremely difficult life. During our meeting with county officials and headmaster Tian Qiang, it was suggested that building special accommodations for the teachers might be a solution. We asked them to draw up the plans and budget and fax it to Beijing. Within six months, Will Go donors had supplied the funds, and six teachers' apartments were completed. That was the first of many projects and mission trips to the area. Then came a big surprise.

There was no visible church or Bible study group. Yet people seemed open to the gospel. One afternoon, a sweet, humble man asked us to his home for tea. He had something important to share with us. When we arrived, he brought out an old, handwritten Bible in the original Wa language. It was reverently wrapped in many layers of cloth. He explained that this precious book was kept hidden (buried) on his land because at different times "such books are collected and destroyed."

How did he come to have this book? God had sent a messenger.

William Vincent Young (grandson of William Marcus Young) from Nebraska, USA, led a group of missionaries in the early 1900s to this remote area with the goal of translating the Bible for the Wa people. The missionaries first had to devise a written alphabet. This rigorous task took several years, but finally, in 1933 the first Wa hymnbook was published. The New Testament followed in 1938. We cannot say with certainty that the Bible we saw was part of Young's work, but it seems highly likely. He must have been an extraordinary young man; history tells us that even the British gave up and left that area because of its harsh and remote existence. But God's soldiers do not give up.

> How beautiful upon the mountains
> Are the feet of him who brings good news,
> Who proclaims peace,
> Who brings glad tidings of good things,
> Who proclaims salvation,
> Who says to Zion, "Your God reigns."
> (Isaiah 52:7)

Our host told us that before the missionaries left, a small Christian group had formed and a keeper of the Book appointed. In subsequent years, China faced many tribulations: international wars, internal wars, and the infamous Cultural Revolution. Seeing this Bible was a clear reminder that God was not finished with this village. He sent us as the follow-up team.

Most of the villagers lived in homes of brick or wood with dirt floors and tin roofs. An open-fire pit used for cooking and heating was in the living room. As we sat on tiny stools around the fire waiting for our supper, we inquired about the black dangling objects above our heads.

"Those are smoked rats," they said. "We'll have some tonight."

Sure enough, we did. A rat, the size of a grown cat, was chopped into minuscule pieces and mixed in the rice. There was no way around it. We ate rat.

Precious hand-written Bible in the Wa language.

We remembered our missions school teaching: No matter the situation, keep smiling. And may we add, be kind. "It's delicious," we told our host. Maybe that explains why a few years later, Li ZhengLan brought us a gift of smoked rat.

My Ride on Jade Dragon Snow Mountain

Life is full of ups and downs, which I was about to experience in an unexpected way. Our dilapidated bus traveled slowly, weaving along narrow dirt roads to reach Yulong County's famous Jade Dragon Snow Mountain, rising 18,360 feet into the sky. We were stunned at the beauty of this majestic mountain range showcased against a crystal blue sky.

Already the farmers had their horses lined up to take us up the mountain to a tabletop plateau. The breed of horses varied greatly, from the LiJiang pony (like a Shetland pony) to the Balikun (like a quarter horse). I (Larry) could already picture myself on the Balikun until we learned the farmers had their own method of assigning the horses.

We were instructed to line up. I was following Helen and Jean when, suddenly, a small Chinese lady jumped in front of me. *No problem*, I thought.

The horses were numbered. We were also numbered and given the horse that corresponded to our number. The little Chinese lady had the number of the grand Balikun horse. I had the tiny LiJiang pony. It was all I could do to keep my feet up off the ground, but off we went. At our first break I asked the lady if we could trade. She agreed. But within five minutes she was waving me down and wanted her horse back. So once again I climbed up on the little pony, but this time, it would not move! Finally, I got off and led the pony up the mountain by the reins. This was not the horse ride I imagined.

A couple of hours later, we reached the plateau, filled with tall green grass and flowers. No matter which way we turned, there were more majestic snow-covered mountain peaks. No brochure could overly exaggerate the beauty of that place.

When it was time to go back down, I asked the main guide if it was possible to get me another horse. He said, "Sure, but you need to pay the fee again."

Being quite conservative, I said, "I'll stick with my pony."

As soon as I threw my leg over his back, he took off like a jet and galloped down the narrow path at full speed. One wrong move, and we would be over the edge. All I could do was pray and hang on. It was clear this was not his first run. Thankfully, we made it down safe and sound.

I often think of that day. It really was a rough ride, but God brought me up and down that mountain safely. It was another incident in my life when God was saying, *Trust Me, Larry*.

I also learned not to take myself so seriously. Jean and Helen (our Christian friend who arranged everything) could not keep from laughing at the sight of me on that pony. I can also imagine the farmer sitting on his stool with rice bowl in hand, half eating and half laughing, telling his family about that big guy on his pony, how smart his horse was, and the jet ride downhill. It's a shame it was before our digital phone cameras. That was one episode worth replaying again and again to give us a hearty laugh when life gets rough.

A Bit of Wa Culture

The Wa are one of fifty-six ethnic groups in China. Their homes border the country of Myanmar, where other Wa tribes live. Li ZhengLan said they had to carry their Chinese ID cards because border patrols would mistake them for Myanmar people illegally crossing the border and arrest them.

The people were hospitable and loved dancing and drinking. Our visits were a good excuse for a village dance. Men and women danced together in a large circle with intricate, choreographed steps. Someone always played a drum, and everyone sang. A table was set up where anyone could get a cup (or cups) of their moonshine liquor. It is said that the Wa may consume more liquor per person than any other group in China. From our observation, this could be so.

When sick, you called the Tax Cho Chai (village healer). The family had to provide a chicken, which he killed, mysteriously "reading" the entrails for the cure. We met this man on one of our visits. Unfortunately, his business prevented him from seriously considering Jesus. This animist practice continues to some degree even today.

We continued to make many mission trips to the village. God was setting His plan in motion.

Li ZhengLan's Story

Li ZhengLan was born in the mountains near the Myanmar border. Her father was a schoolteacher, her mother a tea farmer. She said they were poor; many times they had nothing to eat for days on end. Hunger was a constant fact of her early life. Then it got worse; her father committed suicide. At that time, villagers were highly superstitious and shunned the family. However, she and her little sister and brother could still go to school.

She was only in the sixth grade when the school board recruited her to be a teacher. It was nearly impossible to keep teachers because of the severe living conditions. Li ZhengLan loved learning and was good at organization but getting kids

Village life—dancing, singing, and Tea.

Gourmet smoked rat and tiny stools.

to school was another challenge. The job included going from house to house to wake them up. The villagers did not see the advantages of sending their children to school and preferred their help in the tea fields. It was a hard time, but Li's diligence gained the respect of officials and villagers alike.

> Diligent work gets a warm commendation; shiftless work earns an angry rebuke. (Proverbs 14:35 MSG)

A few years later, she moved to Kunming city and worked at a Cultural Heritage site. She was part of a troupe that danced, swinging their long hair in patterns as they whirled in their colorful tribal dresses. It was an enjoyable season for her. But God was opening another door.

Kunming officials organized a contest to find a girl to serve as their tea princess for a year. They hoped to showcase their teas to the world from their newly opened Tea House at the International Horticulture Expo in Kunming.

Li ZhengLan's beauty, sweet personality, diligence, and quick mind landed her the job. It was amazing how much she needed to learn. Preparation of the tea included washing the leaves, temperature of the water, seeping time, and type of teapot to use. Choosing from the multiple types of tea was another adventure. Who could imagine the medicinal power of a tiny leaf or the multiple flavors and scents? This job was perfect for the little girl born among the terraced fields of tea. God, in His sovereignty, had set in motion our divine connection.

One year quickly passed, ending Li ZhengLan's reign as tea princess. She continued in the tea industry while helping us with numerous projects for the people of her village.

It was about ten o'clock at night in Beijing when I received a phone call from Larry. He was again in the Wa village checking on the new basketball court project when

Larry and Jean with Li ZhengLan.

he heard God speak to his heart. "I think we are to invite Li ZhengLan to come to Beijing and help her get enrolled in college. What do you think?"

I told him that if God spoke it, who was I to say anything but yes?

The next morning Larry asked Li ZhengLan if she would like to come to Beijing and try to enroll in school. She immediately broke into tears. She told Larry that when she was about ten years old, she had this recurring dream that she would live in Beijing and attend university. Only God could bring farmers all the way from Iowa, USA, to fulfill the plans and purposes he had for a tiny tea girl. He never ceases to amaze us. That very week, she returned to Beijing with Larry.

> "For I know the plans I have for you," declares the
> Lord, "plans to prosper you and not to harm you, plans
> to give you hope and a future." (Jeremiah 29:11 NIV)

The goal was to enter the Beijing English Language Institute in the fall, but this required passing a rigorous English exam. Li ZhengLan's sixth grade village education didn't include any English. However, with God's help and her work ethic, that mountain moved. She entered the institute with flying colors and continued to do well. And she shared Jesus. Because of her witness, the fellowship would see another brother.

Meet Xiao Ma

Xiao Ma, a capable young man, was also studying English at the institute and became friends with Li ZhengLan. She continued to witness to him about Jesus and eventually invited him to our home. We'll never forget the day that he sat on our living room sofa and prayed to accept Jesus into his heart.

Xiao Ma, missionary to Morocco.

Xiao Ma grew steadily in the Lord. Today, he and his wife and two small children are missionaries in Casablanca, Morocco. Talk about good ground.

> But he who received seed on the good ground is he who hears the word and understands it, who indeed bears fruit and produces: some a hundredfold, some sixty, some thirty. (Matthew 13:23)

Little Li Goes to Prison

Li ZhengLan's little sister, Li, followed her to Beijing. We encouraged her to join our fellowship and to spend time with Christian sisters; however, she was determined to forge her own way. A few months later, she was caught shoplifting, a serious crime in China.

Little Li was sentenced to one year of prison labor for stealing about seventy-two US dollars worth of cosmetics. Her first job in prison was to make bricks by hand, but when she repeatedly fainted from the heat, she was transferred to another facility. There she packed frozen chicken for export until her release.

We did not forget her. During this difficult ordeal, Larry (though not allowed inside) drove Li ZhengLan and other Christian sisters to the prison with extra food and clothing for little Li. We wanted her to experience and know God's love.

Long before her release, she had decided to return to her village. We were happy to help with the train ticket and gifts for her family back home. Seeds were planted, and even now we continue to pray over those seeds. Today, she is married with a family of her own.

> Then those "sheep" are going to say, "Master, what are you talking about? When did we ever see you

hungry and feed you, thirsty and give you a drink? And when did we ever see you sick or in prison and come to you?" Then the King will say, "I'm telling the solemn truth: Whenever you did one of these things to someone overlooked or ignored, that was me—you did it to me." (Matthew 25:37–40 MSG)

Life Is and Is Not Fair

Li ZhengLan continued to grow in her faith. By outward appearances life seemed good. She had graduated from the institute and was working at a company in Beijing. Then Heidi received an SOS. Li ZhengLan needed help.

The problems started when her wealthy young boss insisted on other "favors" for her to remain on the job. In those days, it wasn't uncommon for out-of-town staff to live in the office. A boss could show up anytime day or night, and he did. When she refused his demands, she was literally thrown out.

Initially she stayed with a friend who tried to talk her into becoming a concubine. It is a longtime practice of China's emperors and wealthy businessmen to keep an unofficial wife. Her friend had an immediate connection. It must have been tempting—her own apartment and plenty of money—but again, she refused.

Not wanting to cause trouble for us or for other members of the fellowship, she turned online, looking for work and a place to stay. That's when Xiao Wu popped up. He was a nice-looking young man in Shandong Province who worked as a cell phone repairman. She went to meet him. Xiao Wu was kind and empathetic, having endured much suffering too. They immediately bonded.

But later, she was back in Beijing on Heidi's doorstep. She was pregnant. It should have been simple; the common practice in China was abortion. But that did not seem right to Li ZhengLan. She believed that she was carrying a life, and Xiao Wu wanted to marry her. But there was another complication. Xiao Wu had a rare genetic problem that caused gradual weakening of all body muscles. Already he had some difficulty walking.

Every action has its own consequence. Thank God that He does not abandon us when we sin or make wrong decisions; He continues to guide and direct us. After much prayer, she decided to marry Xiao Wu. Some months later, they had a baby girl whom they named Xi Xi, which means "double star." Like her mother, Xi Xi (pronounced she-she) is a beautiful and talented little girl. Through the years, the Beijing home fellowship has helped multiple times, buying medicine for Xiao Wu and researching other medical helps.

Li ZhengLan's family will always remain part of the bigger Beijing family though they now live in Yunnan Province where the warm weather is more agreeable to Xiao Wu's condition. Our prayer is that this genetic condition does not pass to their children. Li ZhengLan introduced Xiao Wu to Jesus. Though we continue to pray for his complete healing now, we are assured Xiao Wu will walk in heaven.

> But God demonstrates His own love toward us, in that while we were still sinners, Christ died for us. (Romans 5:8)

Xiao Wu's story reminds us of another young man in Great Britain. At age one, this young Brit had fallen down a flight of stairs and shattered his back. He spent most of his childhood in and out of the hospital. In an interview with Gavin Read, the former Bishop of Maidstone, the boy, now seventeen, remarked that God is fair. When asked if being in the hospital for thirteen years was fair, the young man replied, "God has all of eternity to make it up to me." Amen.

Wang ShiLei

Our motto, "find a need and fill it," brought Wang ShiLei into our lives. The government, depicting him as one of "China's poorest but most brilliant sons," featured Wang on TV, hoping to find sponsorship for his university education. A friend saw the program and called us. "Could Will Go sponsor him?"

Larry immediately said, "Why not? Set up the meeting."

The government had arranged a monthly plan for Wang ShiLei. Larry told him that we were happy to support him, but he needed to come to the fellowship on Sunday, and we would give him the money after the meeting. Yes, the gift was conditional; we were concerned for his soul as well as his mind. At first, he was resistant and detached from the Word. But eventually, God's love and the sincere faith of brothers and sisters in the group touched his heart. He accepted Jesus.

Wang ShiLei was brought up in one of the poorest villages of Shandong Province. His mother had died when he was young, leaving his dad to raise him and his siblings alone. When we visited his home, a huge sack of grain (that year's harvest) was stored in the living room. A small table, cupboard, chair, and bed made up the rest of the furnishings. It was clear that life was still extremely difficult. Larry whispered to me, "There's got to be something we can do here." The words of James came to our hearts:

> What does it profit, my brethren, if someone says
> he has faith but does not have works? Can faith save
> him? If a brother or sister is naked and destitute of
> daily food, and one of you says to them, "Depart in

peace, be warmed and filled," but you do not give them the things which are needed for the body, what does it profit? Thus also faith by itself, if it does not have works, is dead. (James 2:14–17)

We told Wang ShiLei that we would be interested in helping his village in some way. So his dad arranged a meeting with government officials and village leaders. Their proposal for help certainly stretched our faith. They asked for an elementary school. Though on that day we did not have one penny for the project, it seemed right. We asked them to send the plans and budget. Because God raised up so many faithful supporters, the school was completed in less than one year.

Later, we were invited for the Tenth Year Anniversary Celebration. The government had added another room, installed a computer lab, and repainted the whole school. It was such a blessing to see how much they appreciated that initial investment. We continue to be amazed at God's love for all people. Through the hearts and hands of many faithful partners, Will Go has been allowed to bless thousands of children in our beloved China. May every seed sown, grow.

I have shown you in every way, by laboring like this, that you must support the weak. And remember the words of the Lord Jesus, that He said, "It is more blessed to give than to receive." (Acts 20:35)

9/11 in Beijing

We were getting ready for bed when the telephone rang. A doctor friend told us to turn on the TV. "America's been attacked," he said quickly and hung up. We sat glued to the TV and were astonished to see the second plane fly into the

Elementary school built in ShanDong Province.

other tower. It seemed incredulous. Most of the night was spent talking to other Americans in Beijing and praying for everyone involved.

Unfortunately, this nightmare did not dissolve. We began receiving phone calls from some Chinese friends who expressed concern for us "because America will fall now." They seemed to think it was eminent and wondered what we would do. Yes, it was uncertain what the next days or months would hold, but we knew that in this situation as all others, we would trust God. Proverbs 3:5–6 rang in our hearts: "Trust in the Lord with all your heart and lean not on your own understanding; in all your ways acknowledge Him, and He shall direct your paths."

Changes were being initiated around the world. For us in Beijing, a new door was about to open.

Excuse Me? Who's Calling?

The sweet, soft voice on the phone was Ms. Zhu HongYing, a documentary film producer from Beijing Television (BTV). "Your geriatric seminars and work with the elderly have come to the government's attention, and they would like us to film your life," she said. We were astonished. How did they ever find us out of a billion-plus people? It's true that we had done many seminars all over China. It was also true that Larry presented the gospel after every death and dying lesson. With the cameras rolling, could we continue as usual? Did we have a choice? We graciously accepted, and the journey began.

Ms. Zhu, Fan Laoshir, and another gentleman made up the three-person crew. They filmed us at home, in the market, on Tiananmen Square, and of course, during many different seminars. A special bond formed. Fan Laoshir shared that he was a devout Catholic. And Ms. Zhu invited us to meet her

Beijing TV documentary crew.

father, another famous BTV director. It was a joy to drink tea in his home and hear his stories. Through these two, God opened another special door. But it would come with a test.

The Anshan Journey

It was exciting. The McDowell family from Pastor Richard Dutzer's church (New Life Family) had arrived, our China team of translators and helpers were ready, and the train tickets were booked. Ms. Zhu had arranged a Will Go Geriatric Seminar for nursing home directors and leaders in Anshan. Our hotel rooms for the whole team were paid for by a retired army officer.

Our arrival was like none other ever. More than a dozen taxis and leaders greeted us with bouquets of flowers. A welcoming band played music from ancient Chinese instruments ending with the familiar "Jingle Bells." Finally, our drivers wove us through the city past parks, monuments, and a central fountain to our hotel.

We had unpacked and just settled into our nice room when a knock came on the door.

An unsmiling hotel official stood outside our door and informed us to leave immediately. Our free-hotel gift had been rescinded, and since it was a government hotel, we could not even buy rooms there. The officer had changed his mind.

We admit, our first reaction was unbelief and anger. We could choose to get back on the train and go back to Beijing (which admittedly, we briefly considered) or see about other arrangements. We chose the latter.

Heidi and Ms. Zhu scouted out another hotel. Ms. Zhu had arranged for the taxis to accommodate us every time we needed to go anywhere, so they took us to our new place.

The seminar, filmed by the BTV crew, went on smoothly from there. More than one hundred people attended, the

Gift for the military officer—a seed for the kingdom.

gospel was preached, and many leaders learned better ways to care for their elders.

We later found out why the officer had canceled our rooms. The Anshan newspaper had prominently featured our arrival and upcoming seminar. City and government leaders and the taxi company had been given honorable mention, but unfortunately, our army official had been left out of the accolades.

However, before coming we had purchased a thank-you gift for the officer and so asked Ms. Zhu if it was possible to arrange a meeting. We were pleasantly surprised when he invited us to his home for tea. As usual Larry began by asking about family and quickly learned that his wife was seriously ill. Our offer to pray for her was immediately accepted, and we were taken to her bedroom. God's presence was tangible as we prayed for her healing and peace. Later, as Larry presented our gift to the officer, he told him that Jesus is the real gift.

> For God so loved the world that He gave His only begotten Son, that whoever believes in Him should not perish but have everlasting life. (John 3:16)

> For by grace you have been saved through faith, and that not of yourselves; it is the gift of God. (Ephesians 2:8)

The Whole Team—Behind the Scenes

We never get tired of thanking our supporters. Without them, this story would have been much different. When traveling, Larry was able to carry emergency cash to cover almost any situation. Thank God he had thousands of RMB with him and could pay the surprise hotel bill. The real heroes are our faithful "home team," praying we make right decisions and giving so we can follow through with that decision. King David understood this partnership too.

> For who will heed you in this matter? But as his part is who goes down to the battle, so shall his part be who stays by the supplies; they shall share alike. (1 Samuel 30:24)

About two years later our program was aired on Beijing Television. It continued to be shown multiple times and was even seen in some homes in Li ZhengLan's remote mountain village. (Check out the appendix for our YouTube link to see the twenty-one minute documentary.)

Everything was going so well. We loved our life in China.

Educational Helps for Caregivers

We believe the gospel is twofold. First, tell everyone you can about Jesus. Second, do what you can for them practically. Find their need and fill it.

We were so grateful to Mr. Yang, the owner of Tai Shan Xiang He, for allowing us to rent office space inside his beautiful complex. It was built as a mini replica of Beijing's Summer Palace for wealthy elders and was the perfect backdrop for BTV to film our talks and skills. Several elders volunteered to be "stars." Teaching films and seminar clips were edited to create our "Training for the Caregiver" series on DVD. Some nursing homes showed them regularly to improve the skills of their staff. We are so thankful to have had a small part in helping improve the lives of China's elderly. Only God could open those doors.

But in the midst of this, a change was coming—one that surprised, challenged, and stretched us again.

Our Will Go office in Tai Shan Xiang He.

The Vision

Everything was going so well. We continued to hold seminars, our Will Go fellowship was thriving, and we were enjoying our lives in Beijing. But something had changed. During our prayer time, I would see a vision of a neon cross-shaped light over western North America with its crossbars over Vancouver, British Columbia. The vision would not go away. Finally, I asked Larry if God was speaking to him about anything new.

God had been reminding him of a prophecy in 1991 while attending VWMTC missions school in Tulsa. Our group was praying over the western USA. As Larry laid his hands on the map that day, God spoke audibly to his heart and said, "One day, you will live on the West Coast, and you'll get much help from there."

> For the vision is yet for an appointed time; but at the end it will speak, and it will not lie. Though it tarries, wait for it; because it will surely come, it will not tarry. (Habakkuk 2:3)

Though we did not want to leave China, we knew we had to follow God's leading, so we booked a scouting trip to Vancouver, British Columbia. As usual, God was already ahead of us setting up divine connections. Pastor Paul Tucker, president of I AM Fellowship, introduced us to Rich Kao, who met us at St. Regis Hotel on Dunsmuir Street. It turns out he was a pastor and tech guy from Minneapolis, Minnesota; we were farmers and a nurse from Iowa. Though our backgrounds were quite different, our common love for the Chinese people and evangelism knitted our hearts together. We flew back to Beijing and began packing for a permanent move to Vancouver.

About the Illustrator

Jiyuan Guo, affectionately called Ollie, volunteered to digitally draw all the pictures for *Only God*. Because he was living with us at the time (Covid-19 shuttered his university), we were privileged to witness in person the countless hours he devoted to this project.

Ollie was born in Beijing, China, and began painting around age two. Currently, he studies digital animation at Emily Carr University of Art + Design in Vancouver, British Columbia, Canada.

CHAPTER 21

Canada

> **Canada**—Canada has been our home for the past eighteen years (as of 2022). God divinely interrupted our comfortable China ministry with a vision. Jean saw a neon cross illuminating brightly over Vancouver, British Columbia, and Larry was reminded of a prophetic word received many years earlier. God said, "One day you'll live on the West Coast and receive much help from there." No truer word was spoken! We couldn't believe God would send us to such a beautiful and well-cared for country. What bona fide missionary goes there? But God had a plan. The relationships and divine partnerships from Vancouver have literally touched thousands of lives around the world. The good plans of God cannot be overstated.

Though we knew moving to Vancouver was the right thing to do, the devil did not leave us alone. He whispered, "What respectable missionary moves to Vancouver, the city honored with Most Livable City in the World status from 2004 to 2010? Who's going to support that? You'll never have enough money to move there," and on and on. It certainly was a leap of faith, with the cost of living almost four times higher than China, but we knew we had to go.

> But my righteous one will live by faith. And I take no pleasure in the one who shrinks back. (Hebrews 10:38 NIV)

And without faith it is impossible to please God, because anyone who comes to him must believe that he exists and that he rewards those who earnestly seek him. (Hebrews 11:6 NIV)

Will Go, Beijing

When it's right, it's right. Though it was hard to part with people we dearly loved (and still love), it was also exciting. We first met with Heidi and Guo and asked how they felt about directing Will Go, China. They humbly said they would try. The next step? We formed a board consisting of Heidi and Guo, Michael and Chen Jing, Liu Wen and Mae, and Tracy and Chen Mo. They all pledged to help Will Go, go. To this day, they have kept their promise and more.

We thank the Lord for surrounding us with such gifted, hardworking, visionary, and God-loving people. He chose them one by one. All glory to Him.

After this I looked, and there before me was a great multitude that no one could count, from every nation, tribe, people and language, standing before the throne and before the Lamb. They were wearing white robes and were holding palm branches in their hands. And they cried out in a loud voice:

"Salvation belongs to our God,
who sits on the throne,
and to the Lamb."

All the angels were standing around the throne and around the elders and the four living creatures. They fell down on their faces before the throne and worshiped God, saying:

"Amen.
Praise and glory
and wisdom and thanks and honor
and power and strength
be to our God for ever and ever.
Amen."
(Revelation 7:9–12 NIV)

Red Book (Full Payment Deed), Blue Book (Occupancy Deed)

You might remember we had lost our Red Book. Feeling like irresponsible children, we had not told David (the Burden Bearer). Just a few days before a planned trip to the States, David called to inform us it was time to pick up our Blue Book. "Be sure to take your Red Book," he said. Of course, he was shocked to hear we had lost it, having warned us to be careful. However, true to himself, he said, "Maybe I can help."

While we were in the States, David went to the management office and truthfully told them, "They would like me to pick up the Blue Book for them, but since they are in the States, I can't access their Red Book. Is that possible?" Knowing David was the friend who had introduced us, they handed it over to him. At least now, we had half a deed; that Blue Book never left the house!

It was 2004, and God had called us out of China, but first we needed to sell our apartment. Larry prayed and got the figure of money we should ask. No agent was involved—our home was "listed" via the grapevine. Almost immediately we had an offer. But when the potential buyer heard we did not have our Red Book, he cut the offer in half. Larry said, "God told me the figure, so I'm sticking with that." We put out our offer again.

In a few days, our neighbors, who lived below us, offered full price, even when we told them that we did not have the

Red Book. They responded, "No problem," and brought us half the money (in cash) in a paper bag and insisted they needed the Blue Book so they could get the Red Book. We could hear David's warning in our ears. However, reluctantly, we gave them the Blue Book. This meant that they technically possessed the entire deed and could cheat us out of the second half of the money.

We left Beijing to do a geriatric seminar in another province. During the whole week, the devil tormented us with thoughts of *You'll never get your money. Stupid, stupid, stupid.* However, when we returned, our neighbors knocked on our door and arranged to give us the rest of our money. And they had a new Red Book.

Though we had applied at the local land office to get a new Red Book, we were refused. However, our neighbors were able to arrange this impossible feat because of their dynasty relationships. They had lived in the Summer Palace and served the last emperor of China. Some things in China require more than money and cannot be done without *guanxi* (favors accumulated through relationship). But God was not done yet. This dear neighbor, whom Larry had befriended when his wife died (remember "The White Paper Flower" story), was about to receive another gift.

Merciful Miracle—Fall 2014

Ten years after selling the Wang family our apartment, we were back in Beijing with a small team. God placed it in Larry's heart to check on our old neighbor and see how he was doing. As we visited together over a cup of tea, Larry shared the gospel with him, and without hesitation he prayed to accept Jesus. With misty eyes, he told us he had been sick and almost died. Now eighty years old, Mr. Wang believed God had kept him alive for our visit. He called it a merciful miracle.

God's Word is faithful. He told us that he had heard about Jesus as a little boy from European missionaries. Though more than seventy years had passed, the gospel seed remained. Glory to God.

> I sent you to reap that for which you have not labored; others have labored, and you have entered their labors. (John 4:38)

God Will Make a Way
Yes, God will make a way when there seems to be no other way, even when we are wrong. We flew into Vancouver with suitcases loaded with household items, blankets, dishes, and everything but the kitchen sink. We didn't know we had the "cart before the horse." But God.

Oh Canada—Our New Home
After our initial meeting with Pastor Rich, we decided to find a place to live. He recommended a realtor, and we found a two-bedroom condominium in New Westminster, British Columbia. With the sale of our home in Beijing and the radical 30 percent exchange rate from US dollars to Canadian dollars, we had initially secured a loan. We were still in the hotel on Dunsmuir Street when the mortgage company called and said they were sorry, but they had decided not to approve our loan.

In just two days, we were to fly back to Beijing. We needed a miracle. As we were crying out to the Lord, Larry stood up and looked out the window of our room. He said, "There's a bank on the corner. I'll go down and see what they have to say." He took our papers and left. I held little hope of success, but less than an hour later, he returned with a loan from CIBC. He was approved on the spot by a young Chinese Canadian mortgage officer. With the paperwork completed by Jeffry Lowe (the lawyer also recommended by Pastor Rich) and condominium keys in hand, we caught the jet back to Beijing.

Vancouver International Airport—April 2004

A short time later, having said our final goodbyes in Beijing, we were back; a few suitcases held all our earthly possessions. The border officer looked over our passports and said, "Welcome to Canada—enjoy your stay." We took him quite literally. We settled into our condominium and began work with Pastor Rich and his brother-in-law, Pastor Ed Chu. All was going well . . . until it was not. Our innocent ignorance was about to be exposed.

I Could Bar You from Canada Forever

It was four o'clock in the afternoon, and we couldn't wait to get back home. We had been in the USA for a month of itineration and were returning via the Peace Arch crossing at Blaine, Washington. But this time, everything changed. The border officer kept looking at our passport and then finally said, "You need to see an officer inside."

When you are "invited" inside, your passports are checked in at the door, and you sit in the waiting room until your name is called. Finally, it was our turn. The officer did not look friendly, and that was only the beginning. The conversation went something like this:

Officer: "Where did you live before you came to Canada?"
L & J: "China."

Officer: "Where are you living now?"

L & J: "Canada."

Officer: "You cannot live in Canada. You are illegal aliens."

L & J: "But our home is in Canada."

Officer: "You go back to the States and bring me documents of your light and gas bills, rent, and any other proof of living in the USA for at least the past six months."

L & J: "We can't do that; we did not live in the USA."

Officer: "You need a lawyer."

Larry: "We have a lawyer." He proceeded to dig Jeffrey Lowe's business card out of his billfold. Jeffrey's firm had filed papers for Will Go Ministries, Canada, to become a charitable nonprofit, and was working on a work permit for us.

Officer: "Call him."

Larry: "Sir, will you please call him? I have no idea what to ask him. All I know is that the only home we have is in Canada."

With an exasperated look, he grabbed our card and left the counter.

Jeffrey Answered the Phone

It was nearly five o'clock in the afternoon when the officer returned with a smile. "Your lawyer has explained to me that what you call home and what I call home are two different things." He gave us three choices: "I can bar you from Canada for life. I can send you back to live in the USA for a minimum of six months, or I can help you. What do you choose?"

Larry humbly said, "Please help us."

The officer drew up several conditional papers, one of which was to hire a full-time employee for Will Go Ministries, Canada. We can't say it enough. Before you even know you have a need, God provides. Zhang and Diana, from our fellowship in Beijing, had recently immigrated to Vancouver, Canada (with all the proper papers), and Diana was looking for work. She became our first secretary. She had capably helped us in China on some of our geriatric seminars and continued to be a blessing in Canada.

Later that night as we pulled into our condominium garage, we were overwhelmed with the goodness of God. Jeffrey had answered the phone. Without his expertise that day, our journey in Canada could have looked much different.

Living in a foreign land is a privilege. To the best of our ability, we tried to comply with the laws and regulations of that land. We had no idea we were living illegally in Canada. But God had prompted us to register Will Go and begin Canadian work permits. Hearing His voice and obeying brought us across the line and took us back home to our condominium. Even Jesus talked about country rules and regulations.

> Give to Caesar what belongs to Caesar and give to
> God what belongs to God. (Matthew 22:21 NLT)

Redeeming the Time—January 2

"We're here." It had taken thirty-two hours of concentrated driving through a major snowstorm and over unfamiliar roads and mountain ranges, but they made it. Though married for only six months, Jared and Heather Johnson had taken a leap of faith to come and help Mom and Dad develop Will Go Ministries, Canada. And what a great help they were.

Jared created and wrote a Will Go Ministry training manual for mission team volunteers, and Heather completely revamped the Will Go Geriatric Training materials. They spruced up our website and initiated a family cell phone plan. They also helped with the youth and other initiatives at Five Stones Church. But the biggest blessing was family being together.

We had spent much of Jared's high school years away from home on mission trips and at VWMTC school in Tulsa, Oklahoma. Though we knew it was God's timing, we still missed just being with our young son. God, in His goodness, redeemed the time.

> How abundant are the good things
> that you have stored up for those who fear you,
> that you bestow in the sight of all,
> on those who take refuge in you.
> (Psalm 31:19 NIV)

Boiled Eggs for the Homeless

The four of us began our homeless outreach making sandwiches around our kitchen table. Soon after, Pastor Humphrey Tio and his church, Full Gospel Assembly of Vancouver, joined our efforts. We were given church keys so we could use the kitchen anytime. The huge pots were perfect for boiling two hundred eggs, which was Larry's idea to make the meals more nutritious. Music, prayer, and encouraging tracts have been part of this outreach since the beginning. And the good news? The outreaches continue. In 2021, one precious soul received the forty-thousandth sack lunch. But this is no solo effort; some families have been making and donating sandwiches for more than ten years. Faithful volunteers are the grassroots of any endeavor, and we are so grateful for each one. God sees, and He keeps track.

Then she called the name of the Lord who spoke
to her, You-Are-the-God-Who-Sees; for she
said, "Have I also here seen Him who sees me?"
(Genesis 16:13)

Sancta Maria House—Agape Street Ministry

We were introduced to the founders of Agape Street Ministry
in 2005. Though we were not Catholic, we bonded over
our love for Jesus and belief that His redemptive grace is
for everyone. They invited me to be one of the "mothers" at
Sancta Maria House, their home for recovering addicts and
prostitutes. My day was Thursday. It included being there at
seven thirty in the morning to give ample time to organize
everyone and walk next door for eight o'clock mass at St.
Augustine's Parish.

On the first day I served at Sancta Maria, the ladies
surprised me by filing straight to the front row of the church—
their unofficial designated pew. I followed. The service was
always amazing with an impactful homily, special music from
some of Vancouver's finest, and of course, communion. As a
non-Catholic volunteer, I was instructed to cross my hands
over my heart and wait for the priest's blessing rather than
taking the Eucharist (a small communion wafer placed on the
tongue). This went on for several weeks, until *that day*. I was
waiting patiently for my blessing when the priest said to me,
"I will serve you." He recognized the whole body of Christ
and went against church doctrine to include me.

It sounds like Jesus in Luke 9:

Now John answered and said, "Master, we saw
someone casting out demons in Your name, and
we forbade him because he does not follow with us."

But Jesus said to him, "Do not forbid him, for he who is not against us is on our side." (Luke 9:49–50)

After mass, we walked back home, and those assigned to breakfast began preparation. My job was to monitor and teach life skills, help pick up meds with the residents, and offer an afternoon Bible study. But probably the most important job was to listen and pray. The goal of the ministry is that each lady accepts the love of Jesus and begins to follow His plan for her life. Many did just that. What joy!

Larry and Jared and the French Doors
The home needed some minor repairs and French doors installed on the conference room; we volunteered again. Will Go bought the doors and materials, and Larry and Jared did the work. It turned out beautifully and was a functional addition to the home. Serving with Agape Ministry was an inspiration and impetus for continuing to work with people in difficult situations and circumstances. Hence the Wally Project was born.

But First, Goodbye
Two years just flew by. Heather roasted her first Thanksgiving turkey for us. We enjoyed prayer and meeting times, trips to China, serving at Five Stones Church, and just doing life together. It was a vacation chapter for us. God redeemed the time and put a special peace in our hearts. But then came the day when they answered the call to go back to Chicago and serve with Christian Life Church (CLC). What could we say? When God calls, we (they) will go. And so in January 2007, Jared and Heather journeyed back to Illinois to begin a west campus site for CLC. Other events confirmed it was the right

decision for them. And you know our God. He placed them in just the right place to continue to bless and help Will Go, *go*.

The Wally Project

By now we understood that God was exceptionally good at setting up divine meetings. Maria Cook thought it a good idea for us to meet Wally. As he shared his story, a lightbulb went off in Larry's mind. "Will Go Missions should do that too," he told me.

Wally told us that for several years of his marriage, their paychecks only covered monthly bills and basic items. But from the beginning, he and his wife agreed not to run up bills they could not pay. Christmas was so difficult. Each year they explained to their children that they could not afford presents, and none were given. Going back to school and hearing what everyone else had received prompted many tears.

As the years passed, Wally and his wife were more affluent. Their children had married, and they enjoyed grandchildren. That's when they decided to pay December's mortgage or rent for each child, ensuring their families could enjoy Christmas.

So working together with local churches and First Nation leaders, several people were identified as needing assistance, and Will Go paid their December rent. The payment was hand-carried via a friend, the pastor, or us so that we could pray with them and believe God for a change in their circumstances. The Wally Project grew to include many other projects for those caught in the cracks of life.

Battle of the Bands (an Out-of-the-Box Fundraiser)

One of our special events was organized by Keziah Cho and Karmen Wong from Five Stones Church. They knew several young rock bands hoping to make it on the entertainment scene and approached them to help raise funds for the Wally Project. The Purple Crab bar agreed to host the event with the ten-dollar cover charge going to the Wally Project. Fans crowded in to support their favorite band and help them win. Our only expense was to buy a decibel meter. Bands moved to the next round by the sound of their fan's applause measured on the meter. It was a fun, out-of-the-box event for us, and many people benefited.

Nothing just happens; God chooses to work through people to accomplish His plans. We had been working with Pastor Rich Kao since the beginning and saw the church move its home several times. During this season, we were renting the theater inside Douglas College in New Westminster. It was a great location but limited our ability for other activities. We began to dream about ways to reach more people. And then came the Minneapolis team.

The Prophetic

To help clarify each person's role in the body of Christ, Pastor Rich invited a prophetic team from Minneapolis. As they prophesied over Larry and me, they saw multiple ministry helps—just what we loved to do. After all, our motto is "find a need and fill it," using that opportunity to share the gospel of Jesus Christ.

Dream Center, Vancouver

We had heard about the Dream Center in Los Angeles, California; the next step was to visit them. We were amazed at the scope and chain of good works for numerous neighborhoods. And their motto was the same as ours: "find a need and fill it." We came back with multiple ideas, but as in any project, funding is needed. Renting and renovating a building in Vancouver

cost an astronomical sum. Pastor Rich shouldered the burden
and found funding, nothing short of a miracle. Dream Center,
Vancouver, was soon up and running. Glory to God.

We met with the director of Dream Center, Los Angeles,
to see if we needed to pay for a franchise or what paperwork
might be needed to open Dream Center, Vancouver. We were
so impressed with their hearts. "No paperwork is needed,"
they said. "Just go and do it well. We don't have a franchise
on helping people."

> In light of all this, here's what I want you to do.
> While I'm locked up here, a prisoner for the Master,
> I want you to get out there and walk—better yet,
> run!—on the road God called you to travel. I don't
> want any of you sitting around on your hands.
> I don't want anyone strolling off, down some path
> that goes nowhere. And mark that you do this with
> humility and discipline—not in fits and starts, but
> steadily, pouring yourselves out for each other in
> acts of love, alert at noticing differences and quick
> at mending fences. (Ephesians 4:1–3 MSG)

During the next five years, Dream Center, Vancouver,
was the center of activity and offices for Five Stones Church,
Will Go Ministries, and HISG (Canada). Our singular goal
was to bring people to Jesus through community work. We
focused on immigrant neighborhoods, low-income families,
homeless folks, and eventually the world. From this hub we
ran these projects:

Bicycle Safety Clinics (with refurbished bikes for kids)
Carnivals
Vacation Bible Schools

Five Stones Youth Group
Homeless Outreach Prep Center
First Nation Christmas Outreaches
Wally Projects
Visionary Meetings
Free shopping (open daily for people to pick up needed
things or donate items)
Mission Trips (Bella Coola, British Columbia; China; and
Liberia, Africa)
Weekly Prayer (undergirded everything)
Ma and Pa Kettle (Johnson)

Sometimes we laughed at ourselves as we went from place to place, picking up donated furniture, clothing, and all sorts of items with our Chevrolet Suburban, a miraculous donation from the Paul Tucker family. Donated goods were often piled high on top and bulging out the back (Ma and Pa Kettle style), with red flags attached. Most items were organized in the Dream Center (DC) warehouse ready for people to pick up, but we also delivered to those without vehicles. The next story explains many such encounters.

She Was Just One
Late one afternoon, a disheartened young lady entered the Dream Center, hoping we could help her. In broken English she stated, "I don't know where to start, my kids and me. We need so much."

Larry told her, "That's exactly why people donate; take what you need." When we learned she had come by bus, we volunteered the Suburban and let her shop to her heart's delight. But arriving at her government-issued apartment made us cry. She was literally camping out. They didn't even have beds, which had been promised by the government. We put out a plea and, within a few days, were able to deliver two beds to them. They were so grateful.

With each event or outreach, the gospel was shared. We would love to report that hundreds came to the Lord, but we do not know. What we do know is that seeds were planted and that we continue to pray over those seeds to this day. God is the harvester.

> No one can come to Me unless the Father who sent Me draws him; and I will raise him up at the last day. (John 6:44)

> [Jesus said,] And I, if I am lifted up from the earth, will draw all peoples to Myself. (John 12:32)

It's Not a Trick Question

How many bicycles can you pack into a Suburban? Once a year, the Vancouver Police auctioned off unclaimed bikes from their warehouse. Hundreds of bikes were in the lineup, so Jennie Chu, our bike expert, agreed to help us bid. Our heart's desire was to supply new immigrants with a new or refurbished bike. When the day ended, we had purchased fourteen bikes. Larry managed to get them in and on top of the Suburban and back to the Dream Center where volunteers helped with repairs. Through our bike clinics, kids learned bike safety and heard the gospel. It was a win-win. And the bike ministry continues through Kam and Lisa.

Enter Kam Leung and Lisa Wan

Every step of the way, God continued to bring servant-minded, God-loving people alongside to help us fulfill the mandate He placed on our lives. This was also true of Kam and Lisa.

We will never forget a sister's question while on a mission trip to Bella Coola, British Columbia: "Where do you find such people?" The answer: We don't find them; God sends them.

Relationships—Hand in Hand

But how does someone meet two people from Hong Kong living in Richmond, nearly an hour from our New Westminster home? Adrian and Joan Burri, our right-hand couple in China, knew Lisa from their church in Hong Kong. When they learned she and Kam were moving back to British Columbia, they told them to contact us. Nearly a year later, we finally had our first meeting. Immediately God united our hearts, and step-by-step we joined hands for more and more ministry. Today, they head Will Go Mission's work around the world. We remain humbled and grateful for God's divine provision.

Bella Coola at Christmas Time

We had been ministering in Bella Coola for several summers following our introduction to hereditary chief, Noel Pootlass, by his sweet Christian sister-in-law, Sylvia Pootlass. It was late November when Chief Noel called us. "There have been so many tragic deaths in the community," he said. "People are really discouraged. All the teams come in summer; nobody wants to come in winter—but would you?"

Larry said, "Sure, we'd be honored to come." Thankfully, Kam and Lisa agreed to go too. The Suburban was loaded with Christmas gifts for kids; frozen turkeys, hams, and other foodstuffs; also, backpacks with school supplies; new coats; and colorful Christmas tracts.

We set off on a blustery, cold day. Before we reached the halfway point, it began to snow. It grew steadily heavier, and then, to make matters worse, the windshield wipers quit working. Larry tried to fix them but to no avail. We cranked the heat as high as it would go and hung out the windows to swish snow off the windshield by hand. As you can imagine, this plan was not wholly successful. Finally, we reached Williams Lake and replaced the wipers.

The snow had become much lighter, so we made the decision to go on. After all, our heavy Suburban had four-wheel drive. What could go wrong? We were carrying many frozen turkeys, hams, and other perishables for the community Christmas celebration. We had to go.

The second challenge made the first leg look like child's play. We quickly discovered that Highway 20's "low maintenance" sign was an understatement. The road, unpaved at that time, was completely snow-covered. Tall pine trees marked the right boundary, but the heavy snow obscured the left edge of the road, which dropped unforgivingly to the valley below. To say we were praying would be a grave understatement (no pun intended).

Finally, six hours later, we reached the infamous Heckman Pass hill, an 11.2-mile (18 km) gravel switchback descent with many 12 to 18 percent grades. Accidents and loss of life along this stretch are unfortunately common. So with more prayer and care, we began the descent.

Light snow glistened against the streetlamps as we drove through a quiet Bella Coola to the church. With the Suburban safely parked, we leaned back, took a deep breath, and gratefully thanked God that He had brought us safely to our destination. Chief Pootlass and the Prayer House leaders, Jim and Corrine, were shocked to see us. "We thought you'd turn back," they said.

I am the Vine; you are the branches. When you're joined with me and I with you, the relation intimate and organic, the harvest is sure to be abundant. Separated, you can't produce a thing. Anyone who separates from me is deadwood, gathered up and thrown on the bonfire. But if you make yourselves at home with me and my words are at home in you, you can be sure that whatever you ask will be listened to and acted upon. This is how my Father shows who he is—when you produce grapes, when you mature as my disciples. (John 15:5–8 MSG)

Our time of ministry in Bella Coola that Christmas was one of the sweetest ever. Lisa had prepared a video and message on the Father's love. It was so timely and received with tears as God wrapped us in His love. Kids ministry was good too, but prayer times and house visits were the icing on the cake. The Nuxalk Nation needed His touch, and God sent us.

Ministry involves hard work. Many times, the journey to the fun stuff is fraught with challenges, stress, and sometimes danger. Fear wants to grip us, exhaustion sets in, and that "voice" repeating, *You can't make it,* grows louder. But after all, He called us to go to Bella Coola "for such a time as this," and He took us all the way.

Trust in the Lord with all your heart, and lean not on your own understanding; in all your ways acknowledge Him, and He shall direct your paths. (Proverbs 3:5–6)

It Looked Ridiculous . . . But God
We were speaking in Pastor Humphrey's church on the east edge of Vancouver when Larry received a specific word and

instructions from the Lord, which he delivered to the church. "Someone has been trying for years to have a baby but is still unsuccessful. If you will come forward and, in an act of faith empty out your pockets and pull out the pocket flaps, God will show Himself strong on your behalf." Immediately, Mr. Jacinto came down. Larry told him that this seemingly ridiculous act acknowledged that he depended on God to give him a child—that he had nothing left to offer. A year later, Robertino and Cherry Jacinto had a beautiful baby boy and named him Jacob. Only God.

> As for God, his way is perfect. The Lord's word is flawless; he shields all who take refuge in him. (2 Samuel 22:31 NIV)

Barack Obama Will Be President— New Westminster, British Columbia, 2006

I (Larry) had finished paying our car insurance and was coming out of the Kastelein office on Sixth Street. Just across the street, a construction crew was lifting a large concrete slab high into the air. As they tried to maneuver it into place, I noticed a man gazing up at it as if he had never seen such a thing. God impressed on my heart to ask him, "If that concrete slab fell on you, would you be in heaven?"

His response: "Yes, I would be." We chatted a bit, and then as I turned to go, he said, "I have three things I want to tell you. One, the US will go through a terrible financial disaster. Two, the next US president will be a Black man. Three, tell everyone Jesus is coming soon."

Before I could ask anything else, he just vanished. Why God sent an angelic messenger to me, I do not know, but true to his words, the US endured the recession of 2007 to

2009, and Barack Obama became the first Black president in US history.

And finally, remind everyone—Jesus is coming soon.

God Fulfills His Word—2006

Even though we were living in Canada, our love for the people of China did not dim. In 2006, we planned another trip back, not only to Beijing but all the way south to Li ZhengLan's village near the Myanmar border. Several Family Wellness training sessions were planned. Bo and Bonnie Boehning, seasoned troopers, already had their tickets, and we were all set. However, God was not done. Pastor Rich told us he had a friend who might like to join our team. He contacted Kathy Mattson, and she agreed to meet us in Beijing.

Together we flew to Kunming and began the long, arduous trip over path-like roads and mountain switchbacks to Li ZhengLan's home in Shuang Jiang County. The conditions in the village were tougher than usual, even for us. They'd had a long rainy spell. Everything smelled moldy, beds were damp, and mud was everywhere. However, the villagers were very welcoming, and we went ahead as scheduled. The government had specifically asked us to teach on birth control in our women's health workshops, which was a bit uncomfortable since the whole family was present. They clearly had not seen a condom before nor heard of rhythm birth control practices. In many ways, this trip had many firsts.

In hindsight, we had not stressed the difficulty and hardship this trip would entail. To be honest, we didn't know it would be so challenging either. We had endured mudslides in Mexico, rat bites to teammates in Thailand, stinking conditions in the prisons of El Salvador, and other discomforts. But Kathy had not experienced any of this "conditioning." It was a living nightmare for her, and there was nothing we could do to alleviate the situation. With God's help, we slogged through the week; most things went well. The government thanked us for our teaching, friendships were renewed, and more seeds were sown for the kingdom. Now our main concern was to get everyone back to Beijing safely.

God's Prophetic Word Begins to Unfold

Kathy immediately changed her ticket to fly home early. She had come halfway around the world, at Pastor Rich's recommendation, to join our trip. Unfortunately, unforeseen circumstances made it a very unpleasant experience. You can imagine our surprise when, out of the blue, she said, "I've been talking with Heidi and Guo (Will Go Directors in China), and I don't want to see them have to move again. They need a permanent place. I have $30,000 to buy a home for them." We were astounded and grateful beyond words. However, this wasn't the end of the story.

We began looking for homes in the Beijing area. The cost of a nice apartment near the subway had risen dramatically. We couldn't touch anything for $30,000. After much prayer, Larry decided to call Kathy. He asked, "Would it be possible for you to increase your donation to $50,000?"

Without hesitation, she said yes. A beautiful apartment was secured for Heidi and Guo, resulting in a permanent home for Will Go in China. We stand amazed how God works through His body to accomplish His purposes.

God's Prophetic Word Continues

Yes, back to our beloved China again with another team. This time our focus was an evangelistic outreach and a backpack project for four hundred kids at an elementary school that

Will Go had built in Shandong Province. Shortly before we left, Pastor Rich told us his mother, Mrs. Kao, would be joining us in Beijing. He said, "She's already in Asia, and it's a great opportunity to spend time with her three granddaughters," who were already part of the team. We welcomed her. We had no idea, but God was setting things up again.

The Shandong kids captured everyone's heart. Hearts were open and welcoming as we shared the gospel and a song from classroom to classroom and even house to house. It was a precious time—an open window in China. To this day, we continue to pray that every seed planted comes to maturity.

Just a Brick
The only drawback for our Five Stones kids (actually, all of us) was the bathroom situation. There's always something new. The "toilet" consisted of bricks placed about three feet apart in an open room with walls on only three sides. The idea was to step up on the brick and squat. When finished, one had to carefully tiptoe around the other bricks and "stuff" to the outside. Most of us simply could not or would not attempt it.

From a World Tour to a Will Go Team
Mrs. Kao (Pastor Rich's mother) was born in China, but through special circumstances and opportunities, she ended up in Minnesota, USA. Though highly educated and married with a family of her own, she never forgot those left behind. We were on our way home from a nursing home outreach when she asked about our plans for Will Go in China. We shared that we wanted to register Will Go as a Chinese business entity (which would give Heidi and Guo a legal company and status) but still lacked the $15,000 registration fee.

Without hesitation, she said, "I can do that." She went on to say that she had joined our team on Rich's suggestion but was still on a world tour. "I'll send the money when I return to the States," she said, "about three weeks from now." We were again blown over with God's goodness.

Less than a week later, Mrs. Kao contacted us and said, "Check your bank account. I've already wired the funds. God spoke to me during the night and said I must wire the funds now, so I did. It seemed very urgent."

That very day we in turn wired $15,000 to Heidi and Guo. Expecting the funds soon, they had the necessary paperwork ready. Everything was smoothly submitted to the government office.

About thirty days later, Heidi and Guo received notice to pick up their registration. As the Beijing official handed them their papers, he said, "I see you just made it."

"What do you mean?" they asked.

He told them, "By this date and stamp, I see that you were the last ones allowed to apply for a business registration using your own home as the business address. Anyone applying after that date needs to rent or buy another office space."

God had moved on our behalf again, placing God-fearing and obedient people around us. Just as He provided for Abraham in the nick of time, so He provided for us. Jehovah Jireh. Hallelujah.

And Abraham said, "My son, God will provide for Himself the lamb for a burnt offering." So the two of them went together. Then they came to the place of which God had told him. And Abraham built an altar there and placed the wood in order; and he bound Isaac his son and laid him on the altar, upon the wood. And Abraham stretched out his hand and took the knife to slay his son. But the Angel of the Lord called to him from heaven and said, "Abraham, Abraham."

So he said, "Here I am."

And He said, "Do not lay your hand on the lad, or do anything to him; for now, I know that you fear God, since you have not withheld your son, your only son, from Me."

Then Abraham lifted his eyes and looked, and there behind him was a ram caught in a thicket by its horns. So Abraham went and took the ram, and offered it up for a burnt offering instead of his son. And Abraham called the name of the place, The-Lord-Will-Provide; as it is said to this day, "In the Mount of the Lord it shall be provided." (Genesis 22:8–14)

We thank God again and again for all the partners who have come alongside Will Go. Our donors include those living on a small pension who faithfully give $10 a month to those who sow big chunks. However, each gift represents hard work and trusting hearts. For that reason, we remain in prayer, trusting God to show us how to use it or not. Our next place of mission service is Vietnam, and we still stand in awe at how He intervened in Vietnam to prevent a big flush of funds.

CHAPTER 22

Vietnam

Vietnam—Vietnam is a beautiful southeast Asian country with a population of 98.5 million people and is one of Asia's most densely populated countries, with thirty-seven people per square kilometer. It is amazing to see hundreds of motorbikes speeding in a wave down the streets, so close but never touching. However, most impressive is the heart of forgiveness in the people. Though their small country has seen much war and occupation by multiple foreign governments, they remain a gentle and warm people. As one sister told us, "We have much to be bitter about, so we must *choose forgiveness*. Otherwise, we destroy ourselves." Only 8.2 percent of the people are Christians. Much work remains to be done.

July 27, 2009, Hanoi, Vietnam

"I can't come. My father just died."

We were so sorry when we heard the news. Our project partner from Singapore was to meet us the next day to finalize the purchase of our first kindergarten school in Vietnam. But suddenly his father had died, and as an only son, he needed to attend to many things. "My manager will take care of everything," he reassured us.

The next day we traveled to the kindergarten school near Hanoi where, over the last three years, we had taken several teams. We loved the principal, staff, and the precious children in this well-established school. The original plan was to build new kindergarten schools all along the Silk Road, providing Christian training for the young, using this school as a model.

However, our partner had changed his mind and insisted we buy this one first. "It takes time to create new connections and get the paperwork completed. Just start with this one," he said.

And there we were, in Vietnam. Bonnie Boehning had joined us for this trip, and thank goodness. We needed confirmation that we really heard what we heard.

We were all sitting together with the principal of the kindergarten. She was a precious, dedicated young lady. True to himself, Larry first asked about her family and later turned to questions relevant to the school. When he asked about her plans for the school in the coming year, we were not prepared for her answer.

"By the end of the year, I will have made my last payment, and this school will be mine," she said, with a big smile. She related that she had made payments for several years and was so thankful to have her own business.

We were astounded. The business we were asked to buy was 90 percent owned by another! The man serving as the go-between was not aware of this arrangement either and didn't know what to do next. Later, when we tried to contact our Singaporean "partner," there was no response.

Throughout Scripture, God had stopped the sun in its place, parted the Red Sea, spoken through a donkey, and turned water into wine. Couldn't He number the days of a Singaporean father at just the right time to prevent financial harm to our ministry? Though we wanted to continue in Vietnam, no new opportunity arose. God had shut the door.

> The Lord will fight for you, and you shall hold your peace. (Exodus 14:14)

CHAPTER 23

Liberia, Africa

Liberia, West Africa—Liberia has the unique history of being settled by freed American slaves solely for the purpose of evangelizing all of Africa. However, the education and privileges the new inhabitants (USA slaves) possessed began a class divide that culminated in a bloody fourteen-year civil war. In such excruciating times, God arose, miraculously providing the cassava fish for hungry people. Yes, you can read that story too! Though the war raged, the gospel seeds planted by the liberated slaves had taken root. Today, many Christian churches and works still carry that evangelistic fire. We are privileged to partner with them.

We know that as God closes a door, He opens another. We had been asked by Pastor B. Duwah to come to Liberia and hold pastors conferences, but our first priority was to build schools in Vietnam. With that door closed, we looked to Africa.

David Chung, who was working at Five Stones Church, also expressed a love and call to Africa. So together with his wife Erin, we made our first trip to Monrovia, Liberia, in Western Africa. Everything went better than we could imagine, starting with a grand parade, Africa's way of advertising a special event. Pastors conferences, radio interviews, and ministry time in the local high schools filled our schedule. The anointing David had while playing his guitar and Erin's testimony touched many hearts. We knew we wanted to return.

The Cassava Fish, an African Story

This is the story of God's miraculous provision during the seventeen-year civil war as told by Pastor Duwah:

It seemed unbelievable. Every day, we were hungry. The war seemed to go on and on year after year. But we knew if we could get to the ocean, the fish would come. They were so plentiful; we could catch these delicious, meaty fish with our own hands.

After some time, the fish was named cassava fish because, like the cassava plant, it was easy to obtain and could be counted on to sustain us. While the war raged, the cassava fish graced our shores. But as soon as the war stopped, they moved farther out and became much more difficult to catch.

Like the manna for the Israelite children, we knew the cassava fish was God's provision for us. When we needed it, He supplied.

> Yet He had commanded the clouds above, and opened the doors of heaven, had rained down manna on them to eat, and given them of the bread of heaven. Men ate angels' food; He sent them food to the full. (Psalm 78:23–25)

> Then the manna ceased on the day after they had eaten the produce of the land; and the children of Israel no longer had manna, but they ate the food of the land of Canaan that year. (Joshua 5:12)

Bible School—Monrovia, Liberia

> But Jesus answered him, saying, "It is written, 'Man
> shall not live by bread alone, but by every word of
> God.'" (Luke 4:4)

Will Go opened our first Bible school in Monrovia with
Pastor Duwah. He secured many wonderful teachers, and the
school was well attended. Victory Christian Center, Tulsa,
supplied video tapes and other class materials. Other hard-
ware was supplied by Will Go: computer, projector, sound
equipment, and books. Teachers' salaries were paid.

The third year, Pastor Nelson, who was administrating
the school, fell gravely ill. Pastor Duwah took us to pray for
him. At the time, we didn't see any change, but later Pastor
Nelson testified, "From that moment on, I began to recover."
However, due to other factors, the Bible school closed. Yet
God was not finished.

Seven years later, Pastor Nelson contacted us. He told
us, "I never forgot the impact of Bible school on my life, and
I pledged in my heart to open another one. I wanted qualified
teachers and the ability to register with the government. So
I have spent the last seven years, while still pastoring, studying
at the Methodist School of Theology, Liberia. I graduated this
year, and I'm ready. Can you help me?" Today, he continues as
Dean of Will Go School of Ministry, Liberia. Already, forty-
eight students have graduated, and we are nearing another
two-year graduation marker. All glory to the Father from
Whom *all* blessings flow.

> Be diligent to present yourself approved to God, a
> worker who does not need to be ashamed, rightly
> dividing the word of truth. (2 Timothy 2:15)

A Door within a Door

Before we left for our second trip to Liberia, Pastor Dave Kaufman in South Dakota called. He said he had been sending money to Bishop Stephen Lewis in Monrovia and asked us to check on Bishop Lewis. So we asked Pastor Duwah to arrange a meeting. What a meeting it was.

Bishop Lewis was leading several churches as well as an elementary school with about 180 children. Though his old school building had been destroyed during the civil war, the children were still being taught in the church sanctuary. Bishop's dream was to rebuild the school with eight large classrooms. That dream became ours too, and the project was launched. Within two years, a beautiful school was completed, and the kids had a proper place to grow and learn. The new school greatly increased the enrollment, so we began the Children's Food Assistance Program. Each Friday, the children would bring an empty pot or large dish from home. The food prepared was then sent home with them, providing help for the whole family. Hallelujah.

Bishop Lewis became our friend. We trusted him. Through this relationship, Will Go Missions built two additional schools, one in Greenville, Sinoe County, and the last one in Solo City, Rivercess County. In the beginning four hundred children received food on Fridays; with the addition of schools, that number climbed to 860. Thousands of dollars were sent to Bishop Lewis for school building projects, a large latrine, feeding programs, teachers' salaries, an ocean retainer wall, the digging of two wells, and community rice helps. We celebrated a ten-year partnership. Receipts and pictures were sent regularly, and we happily visited the sites every two years.

Is this not the fast that I have chosen: To loose the bonds of wickedness, to undo the heavy burdens, to let the oppressed go free, and that you break every yoke? Is it not to share your bread with the hungry, and that you bring to your house the poor who are cast out. (Isaiah 58:6–7)

Only God Knows

And then some tough life circumstances happened. Bishop Lewis lost his beloved wife of many years; together they had thirteen children. A new wife was selected for him by the elders, the custom of their church. Within in a short time, he remarried. But in 2020, during COVID, his second wife suddenly died. He retreated to his home for mourning. Though oceans separated us, we expressed our love and support of the bishop through compassion offerings for each wife.

More problems arose.

Remote school leaders made various accusations toward our friend and filed legal complaints with local courts. We continued in prayer for them all and contacted Bishop Lewis frequently. Then our usual receipts with their corresponding pictures stopped coming. We continued to pray and wait. After two years without resumed accountability, we had no recourse but to let that door close. Though we do not understand, we know God opens doors and closes doors. We rest in Him.

We WILL GO throughout the whole world, proclaiming the gospel of Jesus Christ to all people, training disciples to do the work of the ministry, so they WILL GO. (Will Go Mission Statement)

CHAPTER 24

Nigeria

Nigeria—Our relationship with this populous African country was initiated in faith by Pastor John Adejoh when he sold his only car to buy an air ticket to Liberia. He hoped to meet us personally while attending the Will Go Pastors Conference. God did not disappoint him or us. We were impressed with his faith, humility, and evangelistic spirit and accepted his invitation to expand Will Go Missions into Nigeria.

Will Go in Nigeria

Pastor John told us that he, too, was an orphan raised by the village widows. One of them shared Jesus with him, and the seed grew. He said, "I wanted to share the gospel, but I had no formal training or platform. And then God gave me the idea to make the bus my pulpit." So for the next few years, he bought bus tickets and preached to the people on the bus. Many were saved. Eventually, he was able to plant a small church. However, he never forgot the widows who raised him and regularly traveled back to his remote village to preach the gospel and bring supplies.

Pastor John Adejohn was an excellent partner. Together, we were able to improve his church building, dig a well for the community, build a six-unit cement structure for women's businesses, and help with food and clothing projects for local communities and remote villages. We also sent rice and new cloth to his beloved widows. However, our favorite outreach was to take the children to the sea, where they could ride horses on the beach. They heard the story of Jesus calling fishermen to be His disciples; they were challenged to be disciples too. In fact, the gospel was always included in each event. Pastor John faithfully sent receipts and pictures. Everything was good and getting better.

Another Helping Hand

Bo and Bonnie Boehning from Minnesota, who helped us so faithfully in China, continued their helping hands in Africa. When Pastor John needed a vehicle, they immediately said, "We have a truck we can donate to him for the ministry. We'll get it to him and include other helps as well."

They sent out a plea for good used clothing, furniture, and other daily supplies. Quickly, their Quonset buildings filled. We began arranging for an ocean container.

But we ran into a major snag. Being new to donating goods internationally, we did not realize that countries have rigid guidelines on what can be processed through their customs. The vehicle Bo and Bonnie wanted to donate was in excellent shape, but it was too old and could not be imported to Nigeria. This disappointing news did not deter them. "We'll sell our truck and donate the money. Pastor John can buy a truck in Nigeria," they said. And they added more funds to give him a beautiful four-wheel drive vehicle.

We felt so terrible that we had not responsibly researched the container business before beginning this project. It was a dreadful mistake on our part. Rather than ditching us and discounting the ministry, Bo and Bonnie chose to have our backs. They lifted us up and completed the project. We remain humbled by such precious servants. The only silver lining? Bonnie was able ride in "her" truck on our next trip to Nigeria.

Our Experience with Nigerian Robbers

Our team was happily driving along toward the remote village where we were to meet the many widows Will Go had been helping. We also had a wheelchair for a special lady who had up to this time traveled in the dirt by her own hands. And Larry still had $4,000 USD in his belt for expenses and projects.

Suddenly, a man came running toward us shouting and waving his hands. "Stop," he said. "Robbers are up ahead robbing the cars. Don't go any further."

Before we could ask what to do, the African ladies were on their knees (in that tiny space in the car) crying out to God for His help. We remained immobile, in prayer for about thirty minutes. And then peace enveloped our vehicle. Pastor John said, "We can move forward now," and we did. We will never forget that scene nor the lesson we learned from our African sisters. Our help comes from the Lord.

Unfortunately, that was not the last time to face the road gangs. Pastor John did what he could to protect us by seating his brother-in-law, dressed in a police uniform, in the front seat. Gang members worked together. One man sprinted out and threw down a plank laden with spikes to immobilize the vehicle. Others hid in the nearby trees, ready to dash out and rob the potential victims. This also happened to us, but with a vastly different twist. The plank had been thrown, but just as quickly, another man from the forest dashed out and picked it up. Suddenly, they all disappeared. Had they seen our policeman? God's protection comes in many forms.

I will lift up my eyes to the hills—
From whence comes my help.
My help comes from the Lord,
Who made heaven and earth.

He will not allow your foot to be moved;
He who keeps you will not slumber.
(Psalm 121:1–3)

Just as God protected the gold being carried back to Jerusalem, He protected us.

On the twelfth day of the first month we set out from the Ahava Canal to go to Jerusalem. The hand of our God was on us, and he protected us from enemies and bandits along the way. (Ezra 8:31 NIV)

No Way

We didn't want to believe it. Pastor John Adejohn's wife, Josephine, called to inform us of his untimely death. He was a great partner and had just begun a new ministry in the state prison. "One man came to the Lord today," he had enthusiastically emailed us just a few days prior to her call. It was hard to imagine continuing in Nigeria without our friend.

Josephine eventually took over the church. Many things were already in place for her provision: church updates, the well, rentals, and a large cash donation for funeral provisions and her expenses.

Pastor John Peter Ogbaje

God stepped in and provided a new evangelistic partner, Pastor John Peter Ogbaje, affectionately known as Big John. "My heart's desire has come true," Pastor Ogbaje texted us.

"I've been praying for years that I could bring practical charity as I preach the gospel. God has answered my prayers."

We began a formal partnership in 2019, but our friendship with Pastor Ogbaje had begun many years before through Pastor Adejohn. Whenever we visited Nigeria, Pastor "Big John" was called to come alongside and help with our teams. His servant's heart was always evident. As we write this account, he and his son Ezekiel have taken the gospel to city schools, remote villages, and into the marketplace. We thank God for their lives and work and pray for His divine protection as they continue ministry throughout Nigeria.

Our African brothers and sisters continue to challenge us with their steadfast adherence to the Word of God. And their harmonious voices and rhythmic music never leave our hearts.

Detroit, the Big D

God's hand was about to move us again. It seemed like another ordinary day in beautiful New Westminster with blue skies and local tugboats chugging up and down the Fraser River. Then Larry said, "God spoke to my heart that America is wounded." When I asked him where, he said, "Detroit." When Larry hears a word from God, we do our best to check it out. We took a scouting trip to Detroit. That trip cemented the city and people in our hearts. New plans began to formulate.

Some Detroit statistics:

- The population declined 57 percent from 1,670,144 in 1970 to 713,777 in 2010. It continues to fall.
- Detroit is considered one of the most impoverished cities in the USA with 30.6 percent of the people living below the poverty line.

- African Americans account for 82 percent of Detroit's population.
- Ford Motor Company is the largest employer.
- Detroit is home to four professional teams: Lions (football), Tigers (baseball), Pistons (basketball), and Red Wings (hockey).
- Triumph Church is the largest in Detroit, though there are multiple other Christian churches throughout the city, with 67 percent of the city considering themselves Christian.

We had been working so closely with Kam and Lisa that transferring the West Canada work to them was seamless. Kam even helped to sell our condominium, which to our amazement had appreciated over 100,000 Canadian dollars. But the hard part was finding a place to live. It seemed we still could not get a release from God to move into the States. So we looked at Detroit's border city, Windsor, Ontario.

> My sheep hear My voice, and I know them, and they follow Me. (John 10:27)

That's Your House

We had only six hours left till our flight back to Vancouver. Our second trip to the Detroit-Windsor area was specifically to buy a house. We allowed ourselves three days, and this was day three. We were beginning to think our plan was flawed. We chose not to call a realtor because we wanted to drive the city and hear from God where to locate.

And then suddenly, there it was. Sitting at 3810 Holburn Street in Windsor was a simple, well-landscaped, ranch-style, brick home. Larry looked at me and said, "That's your house."

Within four hours, our offer was accepted, papers signed, and we were headed back to the airport. God is never too late.

At McDonald's?
We were working with a realtor in Detroit to locate a ministry house. Since we had not met him personally, we agreed to meet at McDonald's. We parked and waited. Sure enough, in just a few minutes, a nice-looking gentleman in a suit pulled up in a luxury black car.

"That's got to be him," Larry said as he rolled down the window. "Are you our realtor?" Larry asked as the man sprayed himself with cologne.

Much to our surprise, he said, "No, I'm Pastor Brock of New Welcome Missionary Baptist Church." We introduced ourselves as missionaries from Canada and briefly shared our desire to help with projects in Detroit. Immediately, Pastor Brock invited us to partner with his church for outreach ministry.

Was it a chance meeting? We don't think so. That day initiated a long-term working relationship.

> If you do what the Lord wants, he will make certain each step you take is sure. (Psalm 37:23 CEV)

A Kiss for Toilet Paper
It was Friday. Larry shared a short message to those gathered at New Welcome Church, who were waiting to receive a box of Forgotten Harvest food. But we wanted to do more. Since paper products were never included, Larry thought toilet paper might be a good, practical gift. We had observed in many areas of Detroit that one scrawny roll cost more than a dollar. Our huge rolls of "Canadian" toilet paper were an immediate

hit. One elderly lady said, "Just what I needed," and kissed me on the cheek.

The Pink Bicycle

Pastor Hill, another kingdom connection, opened his church, Greater Faith for Deliverance (GFFD), to us many times. Together we held family carnivals, Vacation Bible Schools, and holiday events to encourage local Detroit youth in God. During one of our cooperative carnivals, God surprised us all. We affectionately call this story, "The Pink Bicycle."

All our volunteers had successfully crossed the border from Windsor, Ontario, and arrived at GFFD church on Detroit's west side. The actual building was a reclaimed elementary school, perfect for carnival events. Several guys left to hand out flyers in the neighborhood while we set up craft tables, games, the prize "store," and taped colorful posters with Scripture verses to the gym walls. Bicycles of all colors were lined up on a makeshift stage for the final raffle.

At first, only a few children trickled in, but by midafternoon moms and dads, grandmas, and single moms with their kids filled the gym with excited voices. Games were played over and over, prizes carefully selected, and hot dogs eaten. As the afternoon waned, Pastor Hill, with his sweet, authoritative voice, asked everyone to sit down. He told them how much Jesus loved them and gave a simple invitation to accept Jesus in their hearts. Several children raised their hands to receive salvation.

Finally, it was time for the long-awaited bicycle raffle. One by one the bikes left the stage until only the small pink one remained. Everyone was quiet, waiting for the last number to be called. As soon as it was read, a hefty ten-year-old boy (clearly too big for the bike) stood up. Immediately, Larry offered to exchange the bicycle for a bigger one.

"No, don't do that," the boy emphatically replied. "I prayed for that one! All my life I have wanted to give my little sister a birthday present, and now I can. Today is her birthday." With a big smile, he hefted the bike off the stage and rolled it toward the door. We could hardly hold back the tears. God miraculously provided the desire of this young boy's heart. Happy birthday, sis!

Unfortunately, not all our stories have such a happy ending.

We Want to Work

During another Detroit event, three clean-cut looking Black men in their early twenties stopped to ask Larry for a job. "We want to work," they said. "We've applied at numerous places, but nothing has opened."

Sadly, Larry said, "I live in Canada and cannot hire you either." He never forgot the disappointment in their eyes and hoped they were not encountering the prejudice he had witnessed so many years earlier at the Fort Dodge box factory. "I will pray for you," Larry told the men. "God opens doors."

Almost everyone we talked with early in 2020 believed it would be a time of clear and distinct vision. And in hindsight, it was. The global coronavirus disease and lockdowns put us all in positions to stop. Injustice and inequality zoomed to the forefront through multiple events, and we had the time to reflect and pray about those situations; they were not sandwiched between this appointment and the deadline to the next. We believe God used this time to highlight areas needing change, and He Himself is moving the needle toward a fairer system for all. Does this sound high-minded or like so much rhetoric? We hope not. What we do know is that we have committed to regular prayer for righteous justice for all races. And you can do that too.

> Learn to do good. Seek justice. Help the oppressed. Defend the cause of orphans. Fight for the right of widows. (Isaiah 1:17 NLT)

Ministry continued as usual until suddenly everything changed.

Time Out

The GPS said it was right. We had driven around the maze of businesses in this Detroit complex several times but still couldn't see the number of our new accountant's office. Finally, though freezing cold, we decided to get out and walk the area, thinking we had somehow missed the number. And then Larry suddenly went to his knees. I thought he had tripped on something, but he was not moving. Finally, slowly, he straightened up and asked me to help him to the car.

I should have thought my husband had a heart attack and called 911. But I wasn't thinking. His first words were "Give me time, I'll be all right." I chose to believe him. My mind wouldn't let me think that my strong, always can-do guy was not well. We sat there about ten minutes to let him recuperate.

At the same time, we called the accountant's number and found out their office building had burned down. They had moved to a temporary space about forty-five minutes across Detroit (the address was not updated on the internet). Mr. Holden said he would wait for us; just come on over.

It was rush hour in Detroit, and I had only driven in downtown traffic once before. But when Larry asked me to drive, I thought, *Sure, why not?* I should have been thinking, *Call 911.*

Within ten minutes, I missed a turn and nearly side-swiped another vehicle. "Exit, exit, exit," Larry shouted. Finally, I could exit, and he took the wheel. But the surprises were not over. Mr. Holden's temporary office was up two flights of stairs. Larry bounded up as if nothing was wrong. Our meeting carried on another hour, but finally, we were back downstairs and in our car.

Larry just sat at the wheel. "I almost couldn't stand to sit there," he said. "My arms ached so much. I'm not sure what the problem is. I'm so tired."

I laid hands on Larry and prayed a simple prayer, "God help us and heal Larry." We finally crossed the border back into Windsor and were approaching the hospital. "Larry, do you think we could stop and get you checked out?" I asked.

"I'm so tired; I want to go home and go to bed," he replied. But to my relief, he turned at the traffic light and pulled into the hospital emergency parking lot.

We walked into the emergency room together. Larry stood there, fully cognitive, with his usual high color. The registering agent asked him, "What is your problem?"

Larry replied, "I think I had a heart attack."

"How did you get here?"

Larry answered, "I drove."

The next question was "Do you have any pain?"

"My arms are killing me," Larry said.

The man took Larry's health card and asked us to find a seat. They would call us.

The Hand of God

The emergency room was packed. We were among seventy to eighty other folks hoping to be seen as soon as possible. Two hours later, they called his name. The nurse began taking his vital signs and vials of blood while I was supposed to answer routine questions.

"What is your address?" another nurse asked. I was blank. I could not think of our address or phone number or anything. I fought back tears. Larry answered the questions from two meters away. I was so embarrassed. I was the non-functioning wife and former nurse who hadn't accurately diagnosed my own husband's situation. And even now I couldn't help him with simple matters. Please, God, help me.

"Only the hand of God could have raised your husband up," the doctor told me. "Most people with cardiac enzymes this high are not with us anymore. He needs open-heart surgery, but we'll have to find a surgeon willing to take his case. Until we do, he stays here with us."

Late that night, I cautiously and slowly drove home. For the next two days, I continued to be too anxious and distraught to drive. Thank God for taxis.

Two weeks later, Larry was in London, Ontario, for a successful four-way cardiac bypass. Our daughter, Angie, came from Iowa to support us. Later, Jared arrived from Chicago to install handrails in the bathroom and set up a big-screen TV upstairs. Our new normal began.

Recovery was slow. It took nearly a year before Larry regained his full strength, but through it all, we could feel God's peace and presence. We stood in awe as the body of Christ ministered to us with prayer, food, and gifts. We had been given a second chance at life and knew God still had plans and purposes not yet completed. And then the phone rang.

Ethiopian Miracles

Dr. Mikal, founder of Victory Bible College in Ethiopia, called with an invitation to teach in the upcoming fall session.

Because Larry was still recuperating, we of course said no. Not five minutes after we hung up, Larry looked at me and said, "I think you should go." I had not even considered it because we always do everything together. But I felt God's nudging too, and so we called her back.

I was to arrive in Addis Ababa, Ethiopia, on Sunday night at eight thirty and begin a month of teaching at eight o'clock Monday morning. What could go wrong?

The very first flight from Windsor, Ontario, was delayed, which set up a chain reaction of delayed flights. My Toronto flight to Germany had already left, so they placed me on another one, assuring me that I'd arrive in time to catch the Ethiopian flight. Again, too late. At that point, it was Sunday afternoon. I had been traveling for twenty-four hours. The German ticket agency gave two options: overnight in Germany and arrive in Ethiopia on Tuesday or reroute through Turkey and arrive early Monday morning. Of course, I chose Turkey. I arrived in Istanbul as scheduled, ran to the schedule monitor, and nearly fainted. My Ethiopian flight was canceled.

Istanbul, Turkey

The first reality jolt was that I did not have a visa for Turkey. I had to cross the international line into Turkey just to board my flight to Ethiopia. Dragging two suitcases loaded with a month's clothing and all my teaching books, I finally found the visa office and paid the fee. As I again queued up to see about my next flight—and twenty-four hours in Turkey—a middle-aged, English-speaking guy continued arguing with the Turkish officer about buying the "unjust" Turkey visa. He was getting louder and more adamant.

I don't know if I was too tired to rationalize, but finally, I stepped out of line and said to the man, "Dear sir, it does seem unjust, I agree, but there is no other way. You are on Turkish soil. Just go over there . . ." I pointed. ". . . and buy it." He didn't utter another word but whirled around and stomped off toward the visa office. In this queue of about a hundred men, I could see only one other lady. I tried not to cry.

God Sent an Angel

God knows. The young man directly in front of me turned around and said, "I hear from your accent that you are American." He was a young Canadian cardiologist from Toronto enroute to visit his parents. He took me under his wing. Using his smartphone, he repeatedly called Germany, trying to secure my air ticket more quickly. When that was not successful, he stayed with me until it was my turn to book a new ticket and arrange for a hotel. Our next stop was Starbucks, where he bought me a coffee and cake and helped me hook to the internet. I needed to inform the school of my new arrival time and let Larry know I was still alive. Finally, he pulled all my luggage and carried my large, ugly pillow to the taxi. God sent an angel that day and his name was Dr. Refaat Refai.

The Second Angel

It was Tuesday, two o'clock in the morning. The airport was almost empty. For some reason that now escapes my memory, the flight that was to have arrived at ten thirty Monday night was also terribly delayed. My phone didn't work. I had no local currency. And worst of all, no one seemed to be looking for me.

Finally, I decided to venture outside with all my stuff. I stood as close to the door as possible and prayed. Out in the distance were a few cars, but I was reluctant to walk out there by myself. I did not have to wait long. A car door swung open, and a young man shouted, "Are you the Victory Bible College teacher?" I waved back. Immediately, he ran up and loaded my belongings into the car. Off we went to the Victory guest home. He had been waiting since eight o'clock the night before.

"You are my second angel today," I told him. "Thank you for not giving up." His name was Adonias Negash.

"I'm Reading Leviticus, and It's Wonderful"

These were the words of Kumera Wakgari, our gatekeeper: "I'm reading Leviticus, and it's wonderful." He wasn't only the gatekeeper for Dr. Mikal's compound but also my student. Before I was up, he was already reading his Bible under one of the palms. This remarkable young man loved God with his whole being—enough to rough it in a shed and open the gate for anyone, day or night, in exchange for his Victory Bible College tuition. He shared his amazing story with me.

Kumera was born in a remote region of Ethiopia to a prominent landowner. His life was good. Then in his early teens, he was stricken with a mysterious ailment. Over the next few years, all possible medical treatments were tried without success. He continued to deteriorate until he could no longer walk. He said, "Someone had to carry me even to the toilet. I lost so much weight."

Finally, his father turned to the local witch doctor. To secure a potion pouch was extremely costly. His father sold many acres of land. But Kumera told me, "He was willing to do anything to keep me alive."

Several months later, he was lying by the fire in his father's compound. "I felt I was dying," he said. "And then I heard my father talking to the local missionary. She had stopped by many times over the years, offering to pray for me. Always, my father refused."

But that day was different. His father told the missionary, "Go ahead and pray for him. He's dying anyway."

She entered the compound and began to pray.

She simply said, "Jesus will heal you. He loves you."

Kumera said, "Suddenly, I felt like I was choking. The magical pouch around my neck got tighter and tighter. With what strength I had left, I ripped it off and threw it into the fire. Immediately, an ugly smoke arose. My father was greatly alarmed and frantically started shouting at me. He felt I had ruined all chances of healing. But he was wrong. Immediately, I had a strong sense of power, and I leaped to my feet. I had not walked in over a year, and now I could run and jump. Jesus healed me instantly."

He went on to tell me that he asked many people where he could know more about this Jesus, and Victory Bible College was frequently mentioned. He made the long trek to Addis Abba and applied, not realizing how much it cost. Dr. Mikal, seeing his heart and hearing his testimony, offered him free tuition in exchange for being the gatekeeper of her compound. That is how I came to meet this precious young man. Today, he continues to serve God by working at Victory Bible College. God is faithful.

> If one of your brethren becomes poor, and falls into poverty among you, then you shall help him, like a stranger or a sojourner, that he may live with you. (Leviticus 25:35)

More Angels

The students, about a hundred strong, had such a hunger for God. Many of them were in their seats before class even started.

Neriah Muisyo, an amazing lady, was always on the front row—and she was my lifeline. Each Sunday, she and her husband Joe drove thirty minutes out of their way to pick me up for church and then to spend the day. With four small children, it was a labor of love.

And Haimanot Kassa blessed me with visits to her home for freshly roasted Ethiopian coffee. She was my guide at the Addis Abba Historical Museum, where I learned about God's divine intervention in and through the people of this ancient country. I have highlighted some incredible Ethiopian facts discovered from my visit:

- All credit goes to God. One hundred thousand Ethiopians (men and women) equipped only with spears and sticks defeated Italian troops armed with cannons and rifles. How? On the Day of St. George, March 1, 1896, the Orthodox priests carried a replica of the Ark of the Covenant (called the *Tabot*) into battle, praying for all the troops. The fearless wife of Emperor Menelik, Etege Tayitu Bitul, led six thousand calvary to the front of the battle singing, chanting, and playing traditional instruments, invigorating the troops. Against all odds, with God in the lead and unity of purpose, the Ethiopians liberated their homeland.
- Ethiopian historians record that the Queen of Sheba (Makeda) left Ethiopia with a grand entourage to visit King Solomon. She returned bearing his child. The offspring of this union have held rule and stance in

Ethiopia to this day. To carry royal Jewish blood in your veins is considered a great privilege.

- Ethiopia, one of the oldest countries in the world, is considered by many as the birthplace of humankind (Garden of Eden).
- Ethiopia has never been colonized, though occupied by Italy from 1936 to 1941.
- Ethiopian coffee is their largest foreign exchange earner; the country is the second largest producer of maize in Africa.

Here are some Scriptures relating to the above facts about Ethiopia:

And they commanded the people, saying, "When you see the ark of the covenant of the Lord your God, and the priests, the Levites, bearing it, then you shall set out from your place and go after it." (Joshua 3)

Now when the queen of Sheba heard of the fame of Solomon, she came to Jerusalem to test Solomon with hard questions, having a very great retinue, camels that bore spices, gold in abundance, and precious stones; and when she came to Solomon, she spoke with him about all that was in her heart. (2 Chronicles 9:1)

Now King Solomon gave to the queen of Sheba all she desired, whatever she asked, much more than she had brought to the king. So she turned and went to her own country, she and her servants. (2 Chronicles 9:12)

Ethiopians have a strong sense of pride in their country and give credit to God for preserving their land. I witnessed many strong churches and ministries and great evangelism work by Ethiopians to Ethiopians. Truly they are a unique and beautiful people.

Taking a trip to an unfamiliar country without my husband was way out of my comfort zone. I felt lopsided and off-balance. Many times, Larry had said to me, "Use your common sense and listen to God." With each situation, I tried. The following Scriptures were in my heart and mind:

> He who dwells in the secret place of the Most High
> Shall abide under the shadow of the Almighty.
> I will say of the Lord, "He is my refuge and my fortress;
> My God, in Him I will trust."
> (Psalm 91:1–2)

> For He shall give His angels charge over you,
> To keep you in all your ways.
> (Psalm 91:11)

Yes! You can trust God in every situation. Is He asking you to do something seemingly over the top? Do it. Go.

ONLY GOD

CHAPTER 25

Cuba

> **Cuba**—Cuba is a beautiful tropical island, noted for resorts, rum, and cigars. Though it is only ninety nautical miles from Key West, Florida, in distance, it is light years behind in personal standard of living. Many families are without indoor plumbing, adequate electricity, or appliances. And today, food is grossly overpriced and medicine scarce. Through it all, we have witnessed their faithfulness to God and generosity to each other in spite of hard circumstances. By God's grace, our work will continue.

Fidel Castro's rise to power in 1959 kept most Americans from stepping foot on this island oasis. And fear of Fidel's repressive and unpredictable tactics forced many Cubans to flee their own country. Churches were forced underground.

A Sliver of Hope
Then, nearly forty years later, Pope John Paul II visited Havana and held a celebration of mass attended by tens of thousands. Hope ignited again as Fidel reinstated Christmas Day as a national holiday. Gradually churches reopened under new government guidelines.

Only God.

Only God hears the prayers of each human heart and begins His work behind the scenes to bring the answer. He was listening as our Cuban brothers and sisters cried out to Him and began setting up His divine interventions. We believe this was also one of the reasons God took us from beautiful Vancouver, British Columbia, to Windsor, Ontario. Airtime to Cuba is under four hours.

Not only did God move us to Ontario, but He also allowed us at retirement age to become Canadian citizens. Only God could link us through Richard Brochu, a missionary from the Dominican Republic to the Cuban Christian community. And only God, with His sense of humor, would choose an Iowa farmer to bring answers to a few of their prayers. All glory to Him.

> Then he said, "Don't be afraid, Daniel. Since the first day you began to pray for understanding and to humble yourself before your God, your request has been heard in heaven. I have come in answer to your prayer. But for twenty-one days the spirit prince of the kingdom of Persia blocked my way. Then Michael, one of the archangels, came to help me, and I left him there with the spirit prince of the kingdom of Persia. Now I am here to explain what will happen to your people in the future, for this vision concerns a time yet to come." (Daniel 10:12–14 NLT)

What we witnessed with our own eyes were a people sold out to God. They trust Him. They warmly welcomed us into their churches and homes. Pastors and women's conferences, marriage seminars, children's evangelistic events, and health classes were arranged. Beautiful teams assisted us and were a big part of answered prayer.

A Backpack Prayer
Sunday school classes were in full swing as Pastor Yseal led us from room to room to pass out colorful backpacks filled with school supplies. Suddenly, children's happy screams erupted as they ran from room to room, twirling around with the backpacks on their backs. *Gracias, gracias* was heard many times.

We couldn't hold back the tears when a young mother came to us and said, "God heard my prayer. I have two daughters. For years, they have shared one backpack. Just yesterday as I was mending it again, I asked God, 'When will we be able to buy one more backpack?' And today, He not only gave us one new backpack, God gave us two."

> And God will generously provide all you need. Then you will always have everything you need and plenty left over to share with others. (2 Corinthians 9:8 NLT)

A Precious Widow
She still had three children to raise. Their father had been accidently killed when the church roof he was working on collapsed. Our hearts could feel her grief. Pastor Yoel, one of the pastors under Bethlehem Star, told us his church was helping her but more was needed. With joy we became part of that assistance, and two years later, we provided funds for her daughter's quinceañera party. Quinceañera is the celebration of a young lady on her fifteenth birthday and marks the passage from girlhood to womanhood. God placed us in the right place at the right time.

Come to the Water
Pastor Yoel explained to us, "Since we don't have clean drinking water, the government sends a water truck by monthly to

fill our household vessels. The trouble is that we don't have enough vessels to last the whole month." They had been praying for a solution and found that a large fiberglass water tank, big enough to also serve the community, could be set up in the churchyard. But the cost was almost a whole year's salary.

Because of the mighty team of Will Go mission supporters, the money was already in Larry's pocket, ready to be a blessing. On our following trip to Cuba, Pastor Yoel gratefully showed us two tanks. He shared, "As the people come for clean water, we invite them to church. Souls are coming into the kingdom."

> The Spirit and the bride say, "Come." Let anyone who hears this say, "Come." Let anyone who is thirsty come. Let anyone who desires drink freely from the water of life. (Revelation 22:17 NLT)

Are You Kidding? A TV?
We were packing for another outreach to Cuba. The suitcases contained two hundred new T-shirts, multiple bottles of medicines, cases of adult diapers, many new shoes, and more backpacks and school supplies. The value was about $1,500 USD. Just a few days before leaving, an email came from Pastor Yulier's wife. "If you can," she wrote, "please bring us a TV." Our initial thought was *You have got to be kidding. They don't need a TV.* We dismissed the whole idea.

A few days later, we were comfortably settled in a hotel room near the Toronto airport. Our WestJet flight to Holguin, Cuba, was scheduled for eleven o'clock the next day, and we were ready for a good night's sleep. I was peacefully sleeping when suddenly Larry sat up and said, "God said to get them a TV."

CUBA

I was so disgusted. *Why couldn't we have listened more carefully while still in Windsor?* Our car was already in airport storage. Early the next morning, we pulled it out and headed to the nearest Walmart. A small thirty-two-inch TV was purchased and bubble wrapped for carry-on. We raced back to the hotel just in time to repark the car and drag all our suitcases down for the shuttle. The short three-hour-and-forty-minute flight wasn't long enough to fully recuperate. And the fun was just beginning.

We arrived in Holguin as scheduled, piled our suitcases on the trolley, and with TV in hand, proceeded to customs. We had legally declared the TV on our import form, hoping this would speed up any process. Unfortunately, import taxes only began with models as small as forty inches. No one could decide what to charge. Most of the passengers had cleared the airport. We stood alone, waiting for their decision.

Finally, an English-speaking officer told us to pay $240 USD or they would take the TV. Just a few hours before, we had paid that same amount at Walmart. We paid again. As we proceeded toward the door, another officer started pointing at our suitcases. He was saying something in Spanish (which we did not understand—or maybe we did?). But Larry just kept going while waving the yellow receipt in the air. The automatic doors opened, and we were out on the street.

As we later recounted everything to Pastor Yulier, he told us that all the suitcases of another missionary had been confiscated just one month earlier. Suddenly, we realized that God had used a small thirty-two-inch screen to blind their eyes to so much more. He is Jireh. The Lord provides.

> He speaks in dreams, in visions of the night, when
> deep sleep falls on people as they lie in their beds.
> (Job 33:15 NLT)

A House for Pastor Yulier

With each trip to Cuba, we could see the hearts of the shep-
herds and observed their dedication, hard work, and selfless
love for their flocks. In late 2018, God impressed on our hearts
to buy a house for Pastor Yulier and his family. They lived in
three small rooms that ran alongside the church sanctuary.
All five of them slept in one bedroom with a tiny, curtained
toilet in the corner. They washed dishes outside. This was not
the norm; most of their congregation lived in much better
circumstances. We believe God wanted to reward them for
their faithful diligence.

We put out a plea. Within six months, $10,000 had
come in. The new home for Yulier and Janet became a reality.
A sweet footnote was that $2,000 was donated by loving hearts
from our China fellowship.

To say Yulier and his family were grateful is an understatement. God heard their prayers and answered.

> But without faith it is impossible to please Him, for
> he who comes to God must believe that He is, and
> that He is a rewarder of those who diligently seek
> Him. (Hebrews 11:6)

Despite COVID

By now we all know that 2020 locked down almost every
nation in the world. Cuba was no exception, though COVID
was not the only hardship. Scarcity of daily essentials, lack of
ordinary medicines, super-inflation, and the changing of their

currency laid severe burdens on many families. They messaged us to help. "If you can," they wrote, "it would be a great blessing; but if not, we know God will sustain us." Getting funds to Cuba is challenging (putting it mildly) as Western Union, SendValu, MoneyGram, and other usual agencies have closed their gates to her. However, we were not willing to just leave them dangling. Though expensive and difficult, we regularly sent funds to help our Christian brothers and sisters. God always makes a way.

"I Will Go, if You Can Fund Me."

Pastor Luis messaged us that he had a team ready to go. They traveled by horse and buggy and then on foot to remote areas, holding evangelistic meetings and dispersing essential goods and the funds we had sent for countryside pastors. "We were able to bring a renewed hope and joy. Everyone is thanking God and you." Only God makes these things possible.

Bicycle Tires

"My bicycle tires cannot be repaired. I can minister so much more if I can use my bicycle, but a new set of tires cost more than a month's salary," Yulier messaged. What are two bicycle tires to God? Hallelujah, he is on the road again.

A New Refrigerator, Even in COVID

"We bought our first refrigerator. It is a milestone for us," Pastor Alex wrote. He was so excited and thankful that even through COVID, the microenterprise help (start-up chicks, hogs, cement, and building materials) provided by our teams had kept his family and others in food. He did the hard work but witnessed the fruit of his labor.

We knew their story. Twenty years earlier as young newlyweds with a passion for God, they moved to this remote area to plant a church. There was no house awaiting them; they slept together under the stars in a crude lean-to. Through hardship and patience, a thriving house church was established.

God never forgets. Yunia, Alex's sweet wife with her nightingale voice, faithfully leads worship and, through her diligence and hospitality, has carved a home for them within the community. The new refrigerator was His gift to a faithful daughter.

Clip Clop, the New Sound of Ministry

Cubans are extremely hardworking and resourceful. A little help goes a long way. Consequently, when we had the opportunity to buy a horse and buggy for Pastor Yoel, there was no hesitation. Not only could he bring elders and children to church and area meetings, but he could earn extra income during the week as a Cuban country taxi.

Salaries for Forty-five Pastors

Bishop Yseal heads Bethlehem Star, an alliance providing spiritual coverage for more than thirty-nine pastors. They give salaries and other help as possible. With the onslaught of COVID and the other difficulties outlined earlier, paying salaries was increasingly difficult. Only God. He again provided through our donors' monthly salaries for them as well as for six country pastors living near Alex in the Holguin area. God loves and cares for His people.

> Are not five sparrows sold for two copper coins?
> And not one of them is forgotten before God. But
> the very hairs of your head are all numbered. Do

not fear, therefore; you are of more value than many sparrows. (Luke 12:6–7)

You gave abundant showers, O God; you refreshed your weary inheritance. Your people settled in it, and from your bounty, God, you provided for the poor. (Psalm 68:9–10 NIV)

Do not let what you cannot do interfere with what you can do.
—John Wooden, basketball player and coach

CHAPTER 26

United States of America

America the Beautiful
by Katharine Lee Bates, 1893

O beautiful for spacious skies,
for amber waves of grain;
for purple mountain majesties
above the fruited plain!
America! America! God shed his grace on thee,
and crown thy good with brotherhood
from sea to shining sea.

O beautiful for patriot dream
that sees beyond the years
thine alabaster cities gleam,
undimmed by human tears!
America! America! God mend thine every flaw,
confirm thy soul in self-control,
thy liberty in law.

Many years ago, while still living in Beijing, we asked our good friend Adrian, whose homeland was Switzerland, a simple question: "Can you tell any difference between Americans and Europeans?" Immediately he answered, "Yes, Americans *walk with freedom!*"

Though we were surprised at his answer, it highlighted the truth that freedom is inter-woven into the very fabric of our lives. We expect to freely pursue our dreams in science, industry, art, and education. But most importantly, freedom of religion remains a basic tenet of the United States of America, allowing the preaching of the Gospel of Jesus Christ to all people. Our last story reflects this precious truth and still brings tears to our eyes.

From Beijing to Chicago

Boundless Love

Liu Wen, a longtime friend from Beijing, emailed us with an elaborate plan. "Could you meet us in Chicago?" he asked. "I'm concerned about my parents; they are eighty years old now and still have not received salvation. Will you take us to church? I believe God will touch their hearts."

The plan was set in motion. A few months later, on a dark, starless night, Liu Wen; his beautiful, petite wife, Mae; their nine-year-old son, Lan Shan; and his elderly parents arrived on a late flight from Beijing into Chicago O'Hare International Airport, one of the largest in the world. We began the long trek to the car.

We were happily chatting together while moving down the corridor, the only possible excuse we could have for missing our turn. We felt terrible; the elderly Wens were already clearly exhausted from their long flight. But there was no choice; we turned around.

As we retraced our steps, little Lan Shan, with a serious and concerned look on his face, linked his arm in mine and whispered in perfect English, "Jean, next time, just memorize the turn."

I whispered back, "Lan Shan, I would have if I could have; remember, not everyone has a photographic memory like you."

He looked genuinely surprised. "Oh," he said and ran back to accompany his grandparents.

We finally made it outside, and Larry literally ran to get the car.

On Sunday morning, we arrived together at Christian Life Church, Mount Prospect, Illinois, and introduced Pastor Daryl to our Beijing family. When Larry mentioned that Liu Wen was part of our fellowship in China, Pastor asked him to say a few words to the church. No one could have predicted his message and plea.

Liu Wen talked at length about the great love of God and his gratitude for his own salvation. Then he went on to say how grieved he was that his own parents did not know Christ. "Please, I'm asking each of you to pray for them. They are eighty years old. Pray they will accept Jesus soon, even today," he pleaded as he gestured toward them. Everyone could feel his passion for God and the deep love he had for his parents.

Only God knew that on that very Sunday, Christian Life Church would share a beautiful video depicting God's love and salvation, understandable without language; that Pastor Daryl would also preach on the wonder of God's redemptive plan; and that many people would come to the altar to pray. Throughout the service, Liu Wen took careful notes.

Back at the hotel, he and Mae carefully explained everything to his parents. "When I asked them if they wanted to pray for Jesus to come into their hearts, they didn't hesitate a second," he told us with tears in his eyes. "God answered our prayers. How can we thank Him?"

For everyone has sinned; we all fall short of God's glorious standard. (Romans 3:23 NLT)

For the wages of sin is death, but the free gift of God is eternal life through Christ Jesus our Lord. (Romans 6:23 NLT)

But God showed his great love for us by sending Christ to die for us while we were still sinners. (Romans 5:8 NLT)

If you openly declare that Jesus is Lord and believe in your heart that God raised him from the dead, you will be saved. (Romans 10:9 NLT)

For "Everyone who calls on the name of the Lord will be saved." (Romans 10:13 NLT)

CHAPTER 27

Think about This

An ear of corn has from five hundred to twelve hundred kernels, with the average being eight hundred. The current Guinness World Record for the most corn cobs on a single plant is twenty-nine, grown accidently by a retired man in New Jersey (2019). Think of the number of seeds from just that one plant.

Sowing the Word of God is like planting seeds. You may never know how many people will come to the kingdom by the words you share about Jesus. Don't be discouraged. Sometimes the seed is in the ground for a long time before it blooms.

> Those who sow in tears
> Shall reap in joy.
> He who continually goes forth weeping,
> Bearing seed for sowing,
> Shall doubtless come again with rejoicing,
> Bringing his sheaves with him.
> (Psalm 126:5–6)

As you close this book, please join us in this prayer:

Dear God, may all the seeds planted in your name, in any and every place, take root, grow, and bear even more fruit. And on that day, may we meet together at the feet of Jesus. Amen and amen.

Additional Information

Albania

The marble pyramid was the creation of Enver Hoxha's architectural daughter, Pranver, and husband, K. Kolaneci. It was originally intended as a grand mausoleum for her father, who was dictator over Albania for four decades. During Hoxha's time, he either killed or imprisoned roughly one-thirteenth of the population. When we first entered Albania, many people were destitute, with only the clothing on their backs. Thankfully, much has changed, and Albania has recovered in most areas.

China

The Red Guard were gangs of teenagers and university students. Their signature uniform was camouflage fatigues and a wide red band around their upper arm. They roamed the streets breaking into homes, businesses, and schools to obliterate the "Four Olds": ideas, customs, habits, and culture. They destroyed millions of family lineage books, ancient novels, furniture, paintings, and almost anything they deemed evil. Teachers, doctors, artists, and scientists were deemed enemies of the state. Many died in reeducation camps or were shamed into suicide. The cry was "All people must be equal"; the real intent was to create a chaotic environment to bring power back to the Chinese Communist Party. This brainchild of Chairman Mao lasted nearly ten years and was deemed one of the biggest blights on Chinese history.

Dr. Ma never saw her husband again. At the same time she was shipped to southern China, he was sent to the remote north, where he tragically died. Her children were given other assignments too. She could have remained a victim of her mistreatment and wallowed in self-pity, but instead, she chose to serve God. Her love in action blessed countless people. She was one hundred years old when she died peacefully at the home of one of her children. We will meet again, dear friend.

Guo, JiYuan (Ollie)
View additional digital photos by Ollie on our website: larryandjeanjohnson.xyz

Da-Hong Pao Tea
Here's one tea fact for you. Antique Da-Hong Pao Tea can be sold for 1.2 million dollars per kilogram, making it the most expensive in the world. This variety, cultivated from nearly extinct trees, has been declared a national treasure by the Chinese government and dates back to the Ming Dynasty. If you are willing to travel to Wuyi Shan today, you may be able to buy fresh leaves for one hundred dollars per kilogram.

The good news is that there are many types of delicious tea for every pocketbook.

"Red Sunset"
The YouTube link for the geriatric video: https://www.youtube.com/watch?v=MJ7pYjl4GC8

British Columbia, West Canada

The home the Mattsons helped buy in Beijing cost $70,000. Will Go and Heidi and Guo paid on it for several years. Today, it is free and clear and still being used for His glory.

The Mattsons continued to bless Will Go in many ways. For several years they loaned us a vehicle while we were itinerating in the States. This was no small gift as we added eight to ten thousand miles on the odometer every time. Even in dire circumstances, Kathy was there for us.

We had landed in Minneapolis, and Kathy picked us up as usual, except something was quite different. She was unusually quiet. We soon learned that Randy was lying gravely ill in ICU. Just the night before, he had suffered a life-threatening heart attack and was rushed to the hospital. She had left his side to pick us up. Who does that? We remain humbled at the amazing people God brings alongside to help build His kingdom. Randy recovered and helped Will Go, building portable generators for use in remote areas of Africa.

Ethiopia

It should be noted that Yemen also claims the Queen of Sheba.

ORDER INFORMATION